How to Teach Writing, Spelling and Grammar

From research to practice

Helen Walls with Christine Braid

Title:	How to Teach Writing, Spelling and Grammar From research to practice
Author:	Helen Walls with Christine Braid
Editor:	Tanya Tremewan
Designer:	Diane Williams
Book code:	51249
ISBN:	978-1-776559-77-0
Published:	2023
Publisher:	Essential Resources Educational Publishers Limited
	Australia: PO Box 906, Strawberry Hills NSW 2012, ph: 1800 005 068 **New Zealand:** PO Box 5036, Invercargill, ph: 0800 087 376
Websites:	www.essentialresources.com.au www.essentialresources.co.nz
Copyright:	Text: © Helen Walls, 2023 Edition and illustrations: © Essential Resources Educational Publishers Limited, 2023
About the authors:	Dr Helen Walls is a professional learning facilitator and educational researcher, with 20 years' experience of working in schools. She is committed to raising achievement in writing by sharing evidence-based, practical methods to engage every student. Helen is managing director of The Writing Teacher, a consultancy that provides writing workshops and resources for teachers, all accessible online. She is also a member of the Massey University school support team. For her PhD thesis, Helen conducted two empirical studies into the teaching of writing, which included a trial of the Fast Feedback Formative Evaluation System outlined in this book. She has published with *The Australian Journal of Learning Difficulties* and *The Education Hub*. Dr Christine Braid has 40 years' experience as an educator, including 12 years as a classroom teacher and 25 years as a teacher educator with a focus on literacy teaching. In her academic studies, she has specialised in literacy: she has a Diploma of Children's Literature, her MEd thesis looked at using picture books for developing comprehension discussion with older primary students and her PhD examined the influence of teacher knowledge and practice on literacy outcomes for new primary students. Combining her practical and academic experience, Christine works with teachers to promote systematic and explicit teaching and to provide opportunities for incidental learning. Christine has a particular enthusiasm for finding ways to inspire teachers and students using books.
Dedication:	For Mum, who taught me to write and to be curious. *Helen Walls* With thanks to Dr Karen Rhodes, for everything she taught me about the sentence. *Christine Braid*

Copyright notice

All rights reserved. No part of this publication may be reproduced, stored in a retrieval system, or transmitted in any form by any means, electronic or mechanical or by photocopying, recording or otherwise, without the prior written permission of the publisher. Copyright owners may take legal action against a person or organisation who infringes their copyright through unauthorised copying. All inquiries should be directed to the publisher at the address above.

Schools and teachers who buy this book have permission to reproduce the following pages only within their present school by photocopying, or if in digital format, by printing as well: pp 22–38, 75–78 and p 85.

For further information on your copyright obligations, visit:
New Zealand: www.copyright.co.nz, Australia: www.copyright.com.au

Contents

Introduction 4
    Declining rates of achievement in writing 4
    Turning to evidence-based approaches 4
    Overview of this book 4
    How to use this book 5

1. Writing development and general recommendations for teaching 6
    The writing process: a summary of empirical research 6
    The Simple View of Writing 6
    Implications of the research: general recommendations for writing instruction 7

2. Transcription skills 10
    Handwriting and spelling skills are essential to writing success ... 10
    Handwriting instruction: best practice methods 10
    Spelling skills are essential to success with writing 11
    Teacher knowledge for spelling 12
    Spelling instruction: What to teach 15
    Spelling instruction: How to teach 16
    Spelling programme: *Spelling made simple* 21

3. Translation 40
    Teaching vocabulary 41
    Teaching sentence structure 44
    Teaching punctuation use 46
    Sentence structure and punctuation: knowledge for teachers 46
    Sentence-combining for beginners 50

4. The writing lesson 58
    How to use Fast Feedback 58
    Why Fast Feedback works 60
    Key components of a writing lesson 60
    Frequently asked questions 62
    Scope and sequence 63
    Graphic organisers 75

5. Contexts for writing and teaching about genre 79
    Purposeful writing tasks 79
    Teacher knowledge for teaching genre 79
    Using picture books for writing 82
    Weekly plan for spelling 85

References 86

Introduction

Learning to write is essential to success in school. Spelling enhances a student's ability to decode while handwriting helps them to secure letter and word forms in long-term memory. Writing across the curriculum improves students' recall and understanding of new knowledge. More profoundly, writing supports the development of thinking skills, including creativity, logic and reasoning. Beyond school, writing continues to be vital; for example, it is a required skill in over 70% of salaried jobs (Applebee 1984; Graham and Hebert 2010).

Declining rates of achievement in writing

Given how important writing is in education and work, the low rates of achievement across many countries are concerning. In the USA, for example, results from the National Assessment of Educational Progress in 2007 suggest that only 33% of 8th Grade (New Zealand Year 9) students and only 24% of 12th Grade (New Zealand Year 13) students were performing at or above a "proficient" level (Graham and Hebert 2010). In New Zealand, data from the National Monitoring Study of Student Achievement in 2018 indicate that just 63% of students in Year 4, and just 35% of students in Year 8, were achieving at expected curriculum levels (Ministry of Education 2021). In Australia, the National Assessment Program writing data from 2018 show that fewer students are achieving at expected levels for writing than for reading, and that the mean scores of Year 7 and 9 students have declined since the 2011 round (McGaw et al 2020).

Turning to evidence-based approaches

Clearly there is an urgent need to re-evaluate approaches for teaching writing and to identify new methods that work. Significantly, popular approaches to writing instruction over the past 30 years were founded in anecdotal – rather than empirical – research. Now it is time to turn to 'the science of writing' to inform policy and practice. In other words, it is time to consult the numerous international studies that have applied the scientific method to provide more reliable information for educators. It is this scientific body of research that informs this writing resource.

Overview of this book

While this book is research-based, it is also practical and should provide comprehensive support to teachers at all primary year levels. We cover the underlying subskills, as identified in the Simple View of Writing (Berninger et al 2002), including:

- text generation – turning thoughts into words and sentences
- transcription – physically getting those sentences down on the page, using handwriting and spelling
- self-regulation – which means being a purposeful and self-aware writer, able to manage all the complexity of the writing process.

For each of these underlying skills, we summarise research evidence relating to the 'why' and 'how', provide explanations of the teacher knowledge required to teach tricky aspects (such as knowledge of sentence structures) and make practical recommendations for classroom practice. In sum, we hope this book will leave you feeling confident in your knowledge of writing and writing instruction, and excited to teach all the key skills, right away.

INTRODUCTION

Chapter 1 summarises empirical research on the writing process and writing development, and describes implications of this research for classroom teachers. We make a set of general recommendations for developing an effective and engaging writing programme.

Chapter 2 is dedicated to transcription skills: spelling and handwriting. It includes a guide for teaching handwriting, a summary of teacher knowledge for teaching spelling, and routine plans for teaching spelling at junior and senior levels. At the end of this chapter, we set out our spelling programme. This is organised as eight easy-to-follow units, with accompanying assessment checkpoints, supporting you to pinpoint student needs and provide targeted teaching.

Chapter 3 is dedicated to translation, or the grammatical expression of thoughts, which requires vocabulary knowledge and sentence-generation skills. Here, we provide practical recommendations for teaching vocabulary. We also cover sentence structure, including a teacher knowledge section (covering both sentence structures and punctuation use), and a guide to the sentence-combining teaching method – the only evidence-based method for teaching grammar. We finish with a range of advice for helping students to apply their knowledge of sentence structure during the composition lesson.

Chapter 4 is dedicated to the writing (composition) lesson. Here we present the Fast Feedback approach, a set of methods for selecting useful learning goals, teaching to these goals and providing targeted feedback in short, structured conferences. Teachers using Fast Feedback observe significant, positive effects on student achievement and motivation (Walls and Johnston 2021). The chapter offers a scope and sequence, as well as a set of graphic organisers to support student planning and peer evaluation.

Chapter 5 addresses contexts for writing and how to develop tasks that are purposeful and interesting for students. We summarise conventions of structure and style for narrative, informational and persuasive texts. We also provide a list of high-quality picture books that you can use in many ways to support your writing programme.

How to use this book

We recommend first reading Chapter 1 in full for an overview of the key elements of an effective programme. Then you could identify an area for development and refer to a particular chapter for guidance with this. Or you may prefer to read the book from beginning to end and then return to specific sections as you begin to implement the methods in your classroom. Resources such as our spelling programme and scope and sequence may become integral to your assessment and planning processes.

Teachers, your work is so important, and so demanding. We know how busy you are and so we have endeavoured to provide you with reliable information as succinctly and clearly as possible. We hope this resource will become your one-stop-shop for teaching writing and will support you to make writing a highlight of every school day.

© Essential Resources Educational Publishers Ltd

1. Writing development and general recommendations for teaching

Writing requires the use of a variety of motor, cognitive, and affective skills, as we must decide what to say and how to say it; apply handwriting (or keyboarding) to construct a visible representation of our intentions; make multiple decisions on how to frame these intentions into sentences; select just the right words to convey the intended meaning; ensure that sentences are grammatically correct and words are correctly spelled; constantly evaluate and possibly revise the emerging message so it is clear and forceful, and keep working on the message until it is viewed as suitable and persuasive.

Graham and Harris (2014)

The writing process: a summary of empirical research

Empirical research into the writing process highlights how complex it is. To write, we must coordinate many elements, including basic skills such as letter formation, spelling and punctuation use, and knowledge of our purpose for writing and of conventions of genre, sentence structures and text organisation. We must also coordinate the writing processes, including planning, re-reading, evaluating and revising (Berninger 1999; Graham and Harris 1997; McCutcheon 1996).

Significantly, the writing processes do not follow one another in a linear way but interact recursively throughout our composition (Flower and Hayes 1981). For example, skilled writers may evaluate and revise their very first sentence and continue to modify their planning even as they work on final paragraphs. To coordinate all of these demands requires executive function (or self-regulation) skills. This means we are conscious of our purpose and the writing strategies that we can use to achieve it. It means continually re-reading and revising the developing text in line with that purpose (McCutcheon 1988).

Making the writing process even more challenging is that we must manage it within the constraints of our working memory. This memory system is a bit like the brain's 'desktop', storing and managing all new information, and using it in all new learning and problem-solving situations. Working memory is extremely limited in its capacity, particularly for children. As a result, if the student has not practised the technical basics (such as letter formation) to the point of automaticity, these basics will likely occupy all of their working memory and prevent the student from thinking about other important aspects of the process, such as the ideas they wish to express (Berninger 1999).

The Simple View of Writing

So, what do we need to teach in order to support our students to manage this complex process and to achieve their potential as writers? The Simple View of Writing, a seminal model built on the empirical findings on writing development, identifies three sets of essential subskills:

1. text generation – turning thoughts into words and grammatical sentences
2. transcription – physically getting the ideas on the page, using spelling and handwriting
3. executive functions (or self-regulation) – being able to manage the writing process, with intention (Berninger et al 2002) (Figure 1).

1. Writing development and general recommendations for teaching

Figure 1: Overview of the Simple View of Writing – an empirical model of writing development

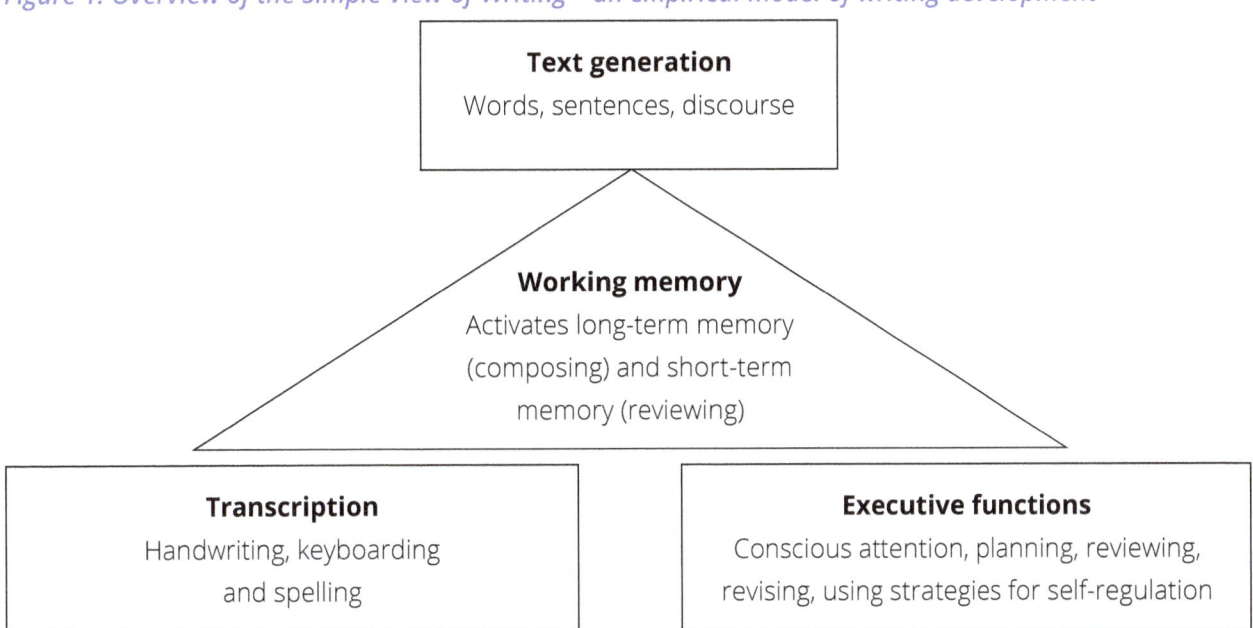

Implications of the research: general recommendations for writing instruction

The following are eight recommendations for writing instruction that arise from the research. Figures 2 and 3 offer evidence from students for the success of this approach.

1. Formative assessment and feedback are key to a successful writing programme

Ongoing formative assessment is essential for targeted teaching. Feedback has significant benefits for writing as it increases students' self-awareness and, in turn, enhances their self-regulation skills. Intervention studies have demonstrated positive effects of feedback, including feedback from peers, although feedback from teachers has the largest effect (Graham et al 2015).

Aim to provide lots of specific and positive feedback throughout the writing lesson. Writing can be challenging, emotionally as well as cognitively (many students feel shy about putting their thoughts on paper for the world to see). Developing writers need lots of encouragement.

2. Explicit teaching is vital

Explicit instruction is effective (Kirschner et al 2006). Teach intentionally to specific learning goals. Be as direct and clear as possible, using explanations and modelling. Provide close support as students begin to practise the new skills themselves.

Explicitly teach writing skills and knowledge for technical and creative aspects. Explicitly teach the writing processes of planning, re-reading, evaluating and revising.

3. Prioritise technical skills, especially handwriting and spelling, in the early years of schooling

For beginning writers, the process of writing a word involves hearing sounds, knowing what letters to write and being able to form those letters on the page. So learning about sound to letter correspondences and letter formation is essential.

1. WRITING DEVELOPMENT AND GENERAL RECOMMENDATIONS FOR TEACHING

Don't ask students to transcribe their own original compositions until they have learnt sound to letter correspondences, along with letter formation, for most single consonant sounds and all the short vowel sounds. Before then, you can dictate sentences for them to write.

The next step is to be able to compose a sentence orally and write it down, leaving spaces between words, putting a full stop at the end and then re-reading to check. Students need to be able write one sentence with a high level of correctness before you ask them to write several sentences or to focus on aspects of genre and style.

4. Confidence with the sentence is key to success

If we can write one sentence well, we can write many.

Teach students about sentences by modelling thinking of an idea and saying it aloud, before writing it down and then checking it. Have students practise thinking of and saying their sentences before writing too, and encourage a habit of reading, checking and correcting (if necessary) after every sentence.

Some explicit work on sentence structure is also important. Teach this using sentence-combining (see Chapter 3), twice a week for about 5 to 15 minutes (depending on the age of your students).

5. We must teach students that skilled writers read and check their writing often

Whole language theorists told teachers that drafting should be a 'free flow' process, so students should only check and edit at a later stage. However, skilled writers read and check their writing often and make corrections 'on the go'. Further, it is very difficult for students to find and correct errors when they have already written more than a few sentences.

So instead, teach students to think of their sentence, write it and check it immediately. They can check it for meaning, sense and impact, as well as for correct punctuation. This is self-regulation at the sentence level and will lead to much better writing overall.

6. Keep the draft book tidy

Because re-reading, checking and correcting are important writing skills, we must support students to keep their writing tidy (and therefore readable). Teach students to use erasers to correct mistakes as crossing out can get very messy. In addition, teachers should avoid writing too much themselves on a student's page: there is little point in correcting every spelling word, for example.

7. Provide opportunities for students to write on a range of topics and for a range of genres

Writing on varied and interesting topics will support vocabulary knowledge. Writing for a range of genres will help students learn about conventions and structures.

8. Establish routines for writing time

Routines and clear expectations for behaviour will support learning during the writing lesson. Pencils, books and erasers need to be easy for students to find. A quiet environment is important too. While it is beneficial for students to talk about their ideas before they write, they should be encouraged to write without talking during their writing practice time.

1. WRITING DEVELOPMENT AND GENERAL RECOMMENDATIONS FOR TEACHING

Figure 2: Comparing writing samples from a Year 1 student over six months of teaching

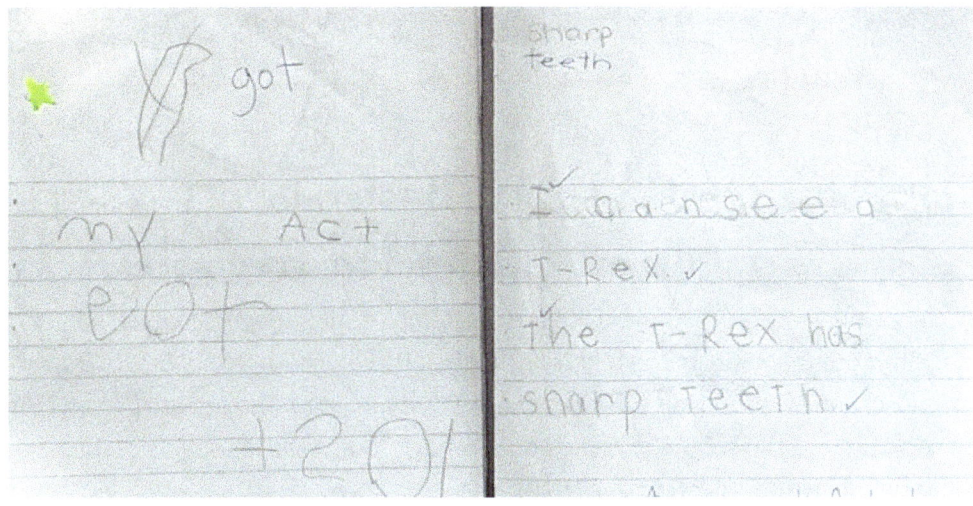

In Figure 2, the student wrote the sample on the left at the beginning of the school year and the sample on the right six months later. Their teacher taught handwriting and spelling every day, and in writing lessons focused on leaving spaces between words and writing in sentences. After six months, the student has these technical skills quite well controlled. They are now ready to write more and to focus on more creative aspects of writing.

Figure 3: Comparing writing samples of a Year 4 boy who struggled with spelling over seven months of teaching

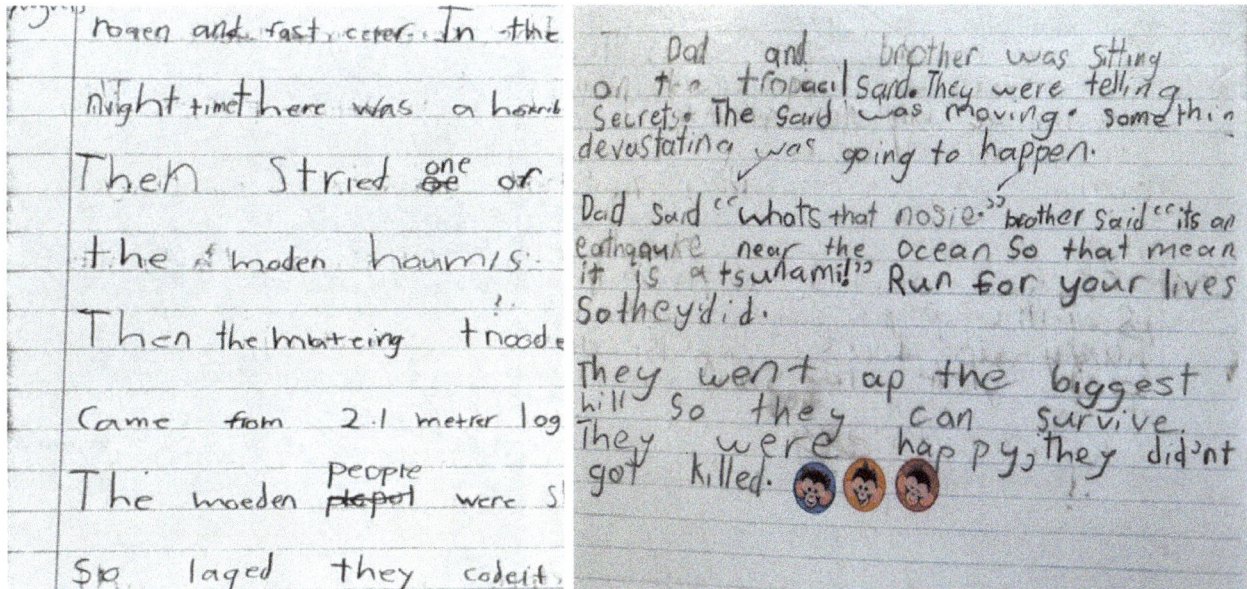

The samples in Figure 3 were collected seven months apart. This teacher taught spelling every day and provided close support to the student during writing lessons – helping him to apply his spelling knowledge. As we see in the sample on the left, this work has ultimately freed the young writer to focus more on the creative aspects of writing, to the extent that he was able to write an exciting story at the end of this period.

2. Transcription skills

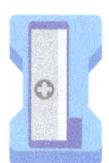

Writing is the way we learn what we're thinking. The handwriting, the sequencing of the strokes, engages the thinking part of the mind.

Virginia Berninger (quoted in Bach 2014)

Handwriting and spelling skills are essential to writing success

In the first years at school, handwriting and spelling skills are the most important underlying factors in writing, together accounting for more than 50% of the difference in the quality of children's stories (Graham and Harris 1997). This is because, until a student automatises these skills, carrying them out will occupy all of their working memory and prevent them from thinking about other, more creative aspects of their writing, such as the ideas they wish to express (Berninger 1999).

The significance of handwriting to writing development cannot be overstated. It is the biggest predictor of writing success for students in the first year at school and continues to have a strong influence on progress in the middle and senior years (Graham and Harris 1997). Difficulty with handwriting often leads to frustration and embarrassment, to the extent that struggling writers begin to hate writing and so avoid writing practice, with the result that they fall even further behind (Jones and Christensen 1999).

Handwriting also benefits reading development, as self-generated letter formation (but not typing or tracing) connects the brain's motor cortex to its speech and language areas and activates the orthographic mapping pathway (James and Englehardt 2012).

Handwriting should be a top priority for teaching, particularly in the early years, or when teaching older students who have difficulties with letter formation.

Handwriting instruction: best practice methods

1. Teach handwriting for 10 minutes every day.
2. Model and describe letter formation for students. Use a set of prompts that is as simple as possible.
3. Closely monitor students while they practise, checking they are using correct formation.
4. Teach students to use the 'tripod' grip (Figure 4).
5. Consider using blackboards for the first months at school. The resistance of the surface helps to develop motor memory and strength. If a student is writing with a short piece of chalk, they will be practising the correct grip (Brann 2000).

Figure 4: Correct 'tripod' pencil grip for a left-handed student

2. TRANSCRIPTION SKILLS

6. Teach letters in their formation groups. These formation groups are:
   - letters with vertical downwards strokes – *l, t, i*; you could teach *f* and *k* as part of this group too
   - letters with rounded shapes, formed in an anti-clockwise motion – *a, d, e, g, o, q, s*
   - letters with sticks and tunnels – *h, n, m*; the letter *r* is formed with the same motions, though we stop at the top of the tunnel
   - letters with rounded shapes, formed in a clockwise motion – *b, p*
   - letters with cups – *w, u, y*
   - letters with sloping sticks – *x, z*.

   You could also teach letters with tails as one group: *j, y, g*.

7. Consider teaching cursive to middle and senior students. Research indicates that benefits follow from teaching both printing and cursive scripts, and that starting with printing and then moving to cursive may be optimal for student achievement (Pulido and Thériault 2022). Cursive lessons may be motivating for older students.

Word processing or handwriting for writing?

Word processing may have benefits for writers who struggle with transcription skills as the text will be readable and is easy to edit (Ray and Graham 2019). However, handwriting helps to reinforce spelling knowledge, and content knowledge, much more than typing does. So, if students are able, they should write by hand as often as possible in their primary (elementary) years.

Spelling skills are essential to success with writing

Spelling is key to success in writing. Correlations between spelling skill and writing quality typically range from 0.4 to 0.5 in the junior years. Even for students in later primary school years, spelling and handwriting combined (together labelled **transcription skills**) account for 41% of the variance in writing fluency (Graham et al 1997).

Other reasons also help to explain how spelling impacts on students' writing quality overall. Evidence indicates a mis-spelled word blurs the writer's message, influencing a teacher's perceptions of the student's ability and intelligence. In addition, if they lack spelling knowledge, a student may avoid certain words – making it harder for them to express their message precisely. Finally, when they experience spelling difficulties a student may feel less confident about their ability to write, which in turn may reduce their motivation and lead them to avoid writing practice (Graham et al 2002).

Spelling supports decoding

Henry (2003) describes spelling as the "linguistic counterpart" to decoding. That is, spelling is a productive process that involves hearing sounds and representing them with letters, while decoding is a receptive process that involves seeing the letters and pronouncing the sounds. According to Ehri (1989), spelling contributes to reading development because it helps to develop students' phonemic awareness (ability to work with sounds in words) and knowledge of the alphabetic principle (the ways sounds can be represented by letters). From there, as students' knowledge of the spelling system grows, they will find orthographic patterns (the ways sounds are spelt) easier to remember.

2. TRANSCRIPTION SKILLS

Taking this perspective further, Moats (1998) argues that decoding should always be taught from sound to print – as it is in spelling. She describes the conventional print to sound approach for phonics as teaching the code "backwards", and asserts that this approach "leaves gaps" and "invites confusion" for three main reasons:

1. The English alphabet represents many sounds in more than one way, and with more than just one of the 26 letters.
2. Many alphabet names bear little resemblance to the sounds they represent.
3. This approach does not "follow the logic of history", in which speech evolved at least 30,000 years before writing, and the alphabet was developed to record speech sounds (Moats 1998, p 4).

Similarly, New Zealand teacher-educator Joy Allcock (2008) urges teachers to work from sounds first. Her argument is that this practice allows us to teach sound-to-letter relationships logically, to acknowledge diversity of sound–spelling relationships and to cover a greater range of knowledge more efficiently – "avoiding the one-letter/one-sound trap" (p 13).

Empirical studies have demonstrated the relationship between spelling and reading, with correlations between spelling and reading ranging from 0.5 to 0.9. In addition, experimental studies have shown that spelling instruction can improve word reading performance (Graham et al 2002).

Given the importance of spelling to writing and reading, it is clear that the teaching of spelling should be a top priority in every classroom. The next section summarises the teacher knowledge required to teach spelling, best-practice instructional methods, and spelling assessment.

Teacher knowledge for spelling

Because many teachers attended school during the 'whole language' era of literacy instruction, they may never have received explicit teaching about the code of written English. This can be a barrier to implementing effective programmes. In this section, we unpack some core vocabulary in teaching spelling (introduced in bold) and explain some useful patterns and rules. You can also refer to Table 1 for definitions of a number of key terms.

This is a necessarily brief introduction to useful spelling knowledge and you will need to teach many more patterns and rules. In the final section of this chapter, our spelling programme, *Spelling made simple*, sets out a more detailed approach you can follow.

How written English works[1]

Spoken English has 44 sounds (**phonemes**). In total, we have 250 ways to write those sounds (**graphemes**) because many sounds can be represented in writing in more than one way.

The **vowel sounds** are made with an open mouth and no friction. They are represented with the letters *a, e, i, o, u* and sometimes *y*. They can also be written with spelling patterns that include consonants (eg, the 'long i' sound, spelt *igh*, as in *light*). Every syllable contains a vowel sound as the 'heart' or 'nucleus' of the syllable.

We teach short vowel sound spellings first as these are the most common and predictable spellings. The short vowel sounds are those we find in consonant–vowel–consonant (CVC) words like *cat, pet, fin, hot, nut*.

---

1 This section draws substantially on Moats (2010).

2. TRANSCRIPTION SKILLS

Each long vowel sound makes the sound of the name of the vowel letter. These sounds are represented by one letter in single-syllable words with no final consonant (eg, *he, she, go*). Usually, long vowel sounds are represented by more than one letter (eg, the 'long a' sound, spelt *ai*, in *rain*, and the 'long e' sound, spelt *ea*, in *beach*).

Other vowel sounds include the *r*-controlled vowels (eg, in *shark, girl, curl, learn, work*); the *ou/ow* in *house* and *down*, and the *oi/oy* in *coin* and *boy*.

Being able to work with vowels is very important for proficient spelling. Most of the complexity in spelling relates to the spelling of vowel sounds.

Consonant sounds are all the other sounds in English. They are made with friction. We touch our tongue against another surface or put our teeth or lips together to make these sounds.

Typical spellings for ...

Short vowel sounds: cat, pet, fin, hat, nut (CVC)

Long vowel sounds: gain, heat, fine, go, blue

Syllables sound like beats in words. We can feel syllables too. Put a hand under your chin and notice that your jaw drops as you open your mouth to make the vowel sound.

We can see syllables in words if we look for the vowel. Then we decide whether to break before or after the following consonant sound (*tea-cher* or *teach-er*).

Sounds and how they are written

Many sounds (phonemes) can be written in a number of different ways. Consider, for example, the different spellings of the 'long i' sound in words like *pie, kite, light, my, buy*.

Sometimes sounds are written with just one letter. They can also be written with two letters (a **digraph**), such as the *sh* in *ship*, or the *ay* in *day*. Sometimes a sound is written with three or four letters, such as the *igh* in *light* or the *ough* in *through*.

Some basic spelling rules

Students can learn certain spelling rules to apply. Most of these are rules for adding endings (**suffixes**) to words. The following are four useful rules:

- Some consonant sounds need double letters (or *ck*) at the end of a short vowel syllable – for example, *puff, will, hiss, buzz, luck*.
- Drop the final *e* when adding *ing* – for example, *smoke* to *smoking*.
- Double the middle consonant after a short vowel sound to 'protect the vowel' – for example, think of the difference between *hop/hopping* and *hope/hoping*.
- Drop the *y* when adding an ending to words that end in just *y* (but not *ay* or *ey*). Change it to *i*, unless the ending (suffix) begins with *i*. For example: *beauty* to *beautiful*, *cry* to *cries*. Note the different treatment of: *monkey* to *monkeys*.

2. TRANSCRIPTION SKILLS

Table 1: Vocabulary for teaching spelling

Term	Definition
Phonemic awareness	Ability to work with sounds and syllables in words.
Phonics	Knowledge of letter–sound correspondences.
Phoneme	The smallest unit of sound in a word. For example, *cat* has three phonemes: *c-a-t*; *shop* has three: *sh-o-p*; *truck* has four: *t-r-u-ck*.
Vowel	We write the vowel sounds with the letters *a, e, i, o, u* and sometimes *y*. When we speak, we make these sounds with an open mouth and no friction occurs with the tongue, teeth, lips or throat (in contrast to the consonant sounds). Every syllable contains a vowel sound.
Short vowel sound	/a/ as in *apple*; /e/ as in *egg*; /i/ as in *itch*; /o/ as in *on*; /u/ as in *up*. These vowel sounds are most common in the first 'little' words students learn to read and spell: vowel–consonant and consonant–vowel–consonant words (eg, *at, get, in, dog, run*).
Long vowel sound	The sounds of the vowel names: /a/ as in *apricot*; /e/ as in *each*; /i/ as in *light*; /o/ as in *over*; /u/ in *use*.
Consonant	The sounds and letters of the alphabet that are not vowels. The sounds are made with friction.
Diagraph	Two letters making one sound (eg, *sh, ch, ng*). English also has trigraphs (eg, *igh* in *light*) and quadgraphs (eg, *augh* in *caught*).
Blend or consonant cluster	For example, *spl, fr, tr*. Although the sounds are not separated by vowels, they are distinct.
Syllable	Each syllable sounds like a beat in a word. It has one vowel sound.
Closed syllable	Contains a short vowel sound and ends with a consonant (eg, *mud*; *pic/nic*). Closed syllables are the most common type of syllable.
Open syllable	Syllable that ends with a long vowel sound (eg, *he, go, day,* **mo**/*tel,* **pa**/*per*).
Schwa	The vowel sound in an unstressed syllable, made when the lips, tongue and jaw are relaxed. For example, a schwa is in the first syllable of *balloon*, in the middle syllable of *family*, and in the final syllable of *sister, little* and *problem*.
Onset	The first sound in a syllable (usually a consonant) (eg, the *c* in *cat*).
Rime	The string of letters following the onset in a syllable (eg, the *at* in *cat*).
Root word	A word with no other parts (affixes) attached to it. The most basic form of the word with a meaning on its own (eg, *start* rather than *restart, starts* or *starter*).
Affix	A group of letters that is added to the beginning or end of a root word and has a meaning of its own. An affix changes the meaning of the root word.
Prefix	A word part that is added to the beginning of a root word and has a meaning of its own (eg, *dis-, pre-, uni-*). A prefix changes the meaning of the root word (eg, *disappear* is the opposite of *appear*).
Suffix	A word part that is added to the end of a root word and has a meaning of its own (eg, *-able, -est, -ful*). A suffix changes the meaning and grammatical function of the root word (eg, compare *adapt* and *adaptable*).

2. TRANSCRIPTION SKILLS

Spelling instruction: What to teach

A number of researchers have described spelling development on a continuum from learning to work with sounds (**phonological awareness**), to learning how these sounds are represented by letters (**alphabetic principle**), to learning about word structures and meaningful word parts (**morphology**) and word origins (**etymology**). On this basis, the following are the priorities for teaching:

- Teach phonemic awareness (the ability to hear sounds and syllables in words).
- Teach sound to letter patterns and relevant spelling rules.
- Work on lists of words with the same sound to letter correspondences (not randomly spelt 'essential words').
- Teach about word structures. For example, explain the ways that prefixes and suffixes can be added to words and how they change word meanings (such as the *un* in *unkind*).
- Teach about words origins when this knowledge is relevant and interesting. For example, the *kn* in *know* and *knife* has come from the Germanic-speaking tribes who invaded the British Isles from 400 AD.
- Teach students the meanings of Latin and Greek roots and how to work with them. For example, the Latin root *rupt* means to break or burst, and appears in words like *erupt, eruption, disrupt, disrupted* and *rupture*. See Table 2 for a list of common Latin and Greek roots, prefixes and suffixes.

Table 2: Common roots and affixes to teach

Prefixes and their meanings					
a-, ab-, abs-	away, from	*di-, dif-, dis-*	apart, in different directions, not	*poly-*	many
anti-	against			*pre-*	before
ad-	to, toward, add to	*ex-*	out	*pro-*	forward, ahead
		for-	away/against	*re-*	back, again
circu-	around	*fore-*	before, ahead	*sub-*	under, below
co-, com-, con-, col-	with, together	*in-, im-, il-*	in, on, into, not	*tra-, tran-, trans-*	across, change
		mis-	wrongly		
contra-	against	*multi-*	many	*un-*	not
de-	off, away	*out-*	beyond	*under-*	below
Suffixes and how they mark the grammatical function of a word					
-ed	past tense verb	*-less*	adjective	*-er*	comparative adjective
-ly, -y	adverb	*-ness*	noun	*-est*	superlative adjective
-ful	quantity noun or adjective	*-ing*	present, continuous verb	*-hood*	noun
				-ish	adjective
Latin and Greek roots and their meanings					
andr	human	*geo*	earth	*pon, pos, posit*	put, place
audi	hear, listen	*graph, gram*	write, draw	*port*	carry
chron	time	*hemi*	half	*rupt*	burst, break
cred	believe	*ject*	throw, cast	*scrib, script*	write
cur, curs, cours	run, go	*mono*	one	*spect*	see
dem	people	*mis, mit*	send	*sphere*	ball
dict	say, tell, speak	*mov, mot, mobil*	move	*tele*	far, distant
duc, duct	lead	*path*	disease	*terr*	earth
fac, fic, fact, fect	do, make	*phobia*	fear	*vid, vis*	see

Source: Adapted from Van Cleave (2019) and Wilfong (2021).

2. TRANSCRIPTION SKILLS

Spelling instruction: How to teach

Work from sounds first

We should support students to analyse the sounds in words before they learn to spell them. As discussed on page 12, Moats has given some convincing reasons for this approach. The following are some further reasons:

- Students come to school knowing more about spoken language and sounds than they do about print. When we work from sounds first, we are connecting new knowledge with prior knowledge.
- We can use the sounds in words as a trigger for recalling spellings. To use an analogy, we can use the 44 sounds of English as we would labels on a filing cabinet, helping us to retrieve the information easily.
- Sound analysis will continue to be useful to advanced spellers, whenever they are required to write a word that is unfamiliar to them (Allcock 2008; Brann 2001).

Acknowledge that English spelling is diverse as most sounds can be written in different ways

For example, if we tell our students, "*e is for egg*", this will confuse them when they encounter words such as *make*, *pear* and *each*. Instead, express it in a way that recognises other possibilities, such as "*e* **can** represent the sound ..." (Brann 2001; Joshi et al 2008).

"*E can represent the sound in egg.*"

Multisensory activities are effective

Connecting auditory (sound), visual (print) and kinaesthetic (touch) aspects of learning will aid with memory and will make learning fun for students who love to move (Brann 2001; Henry 2003).

Here are some ideas for multisensory activities:

- Use a palm sweep from left to right to show when sounds change in words. For example, if segmenting the word *cat*, you would start with your palm facing outwards, then move it inwards and then outwards again as you articulate the three sounds.
- Use 'spelling fingers' to count sounds. Hold your hand in the air and pop your fingers up from left to right as the sounds change.
- Use playdough worms. Make indentations for each phoneme. Then roll these worms into word snails and blend the sounds back together.
- Use poppets to segment sound.
- Record words in Elkonin boxes – each box represents one sound (Figure 5).
- Clap and dance to syllables.

Figure 5: Working with Elkonin boxes

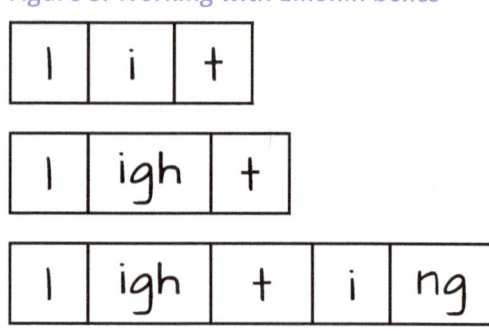

Teach spelling 'little and often'

Teaching little and often is a well-established principle to help all learning 'stick'. Students need to practise retrieving knowledge from memory before they completely forget it; otherwise you will need to teach the same topic all over again. So 10 minutes of spelling instruction every day will be more effective than longer lessons once or twice a week (Jones et al 2006).

What about memorisation?

Teaching students about sound to letter correspondences and word structures makes spellings more memorable. It also allows them to learn words as groups, rather than as individual units. Memorising individual words is inefficient and would make it impossible to cover the 70,000 words that literate adults need to know (Graham et al 2002; Stone 2021).

What about invented spelling?

Whole language theorists recommended that students listen to sounds to approximate spellings while writing. This can be problematic, especially when students need to record sounds where the spelling is unpredictable. In this case, students will either record the sound incorrectly, or (in a worst-case scenario) become anxious about guessing at the word and making a mistake.

Henry (2003) urges teachers to explicitly teach sound to letter correspondences to enable students to spell words correctly as soon as possible. We recommend using a 'supported spelling' routine, in which teachers help the student to listen to sounds, encourage them to apply the knowledge they have, and show them the rest of the word.

Spelling routine

In a junior class, teach a whole-class lesson for about 10 minutes every day. In the first six months, focus on hearing sounds in words. Later, put a greater emphasis on writing the sounds. Exhibit 1 sets out a suggested routine for teaching phonemic awareness and spelling to junior students.

In a middle or senior class, teach for 15–20 minutes a day. This could be a whole-class lesson if you have more targeted instruction in sound–letter patterns as a part of your reading routine. Exhibit 2 sets out a suggested weekly routine for teaching spelling in middle and senior schools.

Target these lessons to meet the needs of students at the earlier stages of spelling development. More proficient spellers will benefit from revision. Revisit sound–letter patterns later in the day when you teach reading. If you teach in reading groups, you can extend more proficient spellers during this small group time.

2. TRANSCRIPTION SKILLS

Exhibit 1: Ten-minute lesson with toys – junior school

Use this lesson to teach early sound–letter correspondences, including short vowel and single consonant sounds, and early digraphs (*sh, ch, th, ng, ph, ck*). Teach the skills: segmenting, blending, phoneme manipulation and syllable identification (Brann 2001; Joshi et al 2008).

You will need to collect a number of toys or picture cards representing CVC, CCVC or CVCC words (eg, pig, peg, dog, jet, frog, fish, ring, chips). Some other toys may be useful for just their initial sound and to provide opportunities to practise hearing more than one syllable (an apple for the 'short a' or a panther for the digraph /th/).

Choose three cards or toys a day for practising the following skills. Choose just two activities to use each day during this whole-class time. Include more focused phonemic awareness work when teaching groups during your reading session.

1. **Segment words to identify initial, medial or final sounds.** For example, say, "Which toys have a /f/ at the beginning? The f-i-sh? The f-r-o-g? The c-a-t?" Record the words after segmenting them and discuss the recording of the target sound (for the above example, *f*).

2. **Blend sounds to make a word.** The teacher segments and the students blend the sounds together to say a word.

   Say, "I am thinking of a toy. I will make the sounds. You put the sounds together and tell me what the word is: d-o-g." Record the words after blending them.

3. **Manipulate phonemes.** Show the students a toy (eg, a jet) and record the word on the whiteboard.

   Say, "This word says *jet*. How can I make it say *pet*? What letter should I rub out? What letter should I write now?"

   You could repeat this for a few different changes, including changes to the medial and final sounds: *jet, pet, pot, pat, fat, fan, fin*.

4. **Identify syllables.** Do this at the end of your lesson every day, as it gives students an opportunity to move about. Put the toys in the middle of the circle.

   Say, "We can hear beats in words. The beats are called syllables."

   Then support students to say, clap and dance to the names of the toys.

   You can also say a sentence about one of the toys, and students can clap and dance to the sentence too (read more about this in Chapter 3).

Note: Thanks to Barbara Brann for the basis for this activity.

2. TRANSCRIPTION SKILLS

2. TRANSCRIPTION SKILLS

Exhibit 2: Ten minutes a day, from Monday to Friday – middle and senior school

Day 1: Introduce the sound or rule for the week

- Work with your class to create a list of words with that sound or rule. Segment and spell words as the students suggest them.
- For many sounds, you may end up with a list of words with several different spelling patterns (eg, for the 'long a' sound, *rain, day, frame, great, eight*). Read the list and talk about the different ways the sound can be spelt.
- Choose one spelling pattern to focus on for the week. Save other patterns for following weeks.

Day 2: Focus on word meanings

Re-read the list as a class. Remind students of the focus pattern or rule.

- Choose two or three words from the list. Discuss them in relation to one of these topics: the meanings of interesting words; changing the words by adding endings (*swimming, swimmer*); or changing them by changing tenses (*swim, swam*).
- At this stage, don't dwell on labelling word parts (eg, prefix, suffix) or parts of speech (eg, verb, noun) as this can reduce students' confidence and motivation. Instead, build students' consciousness of and curiosity about words. Encourage them to explain changes to meanings and tenses using their own words. Praise questions about these complex concepts.

Follow-up: Students could write their own definitions or put the words into sentences to show their meanings. They could create a 'word map' showing everything they know about a particular word.

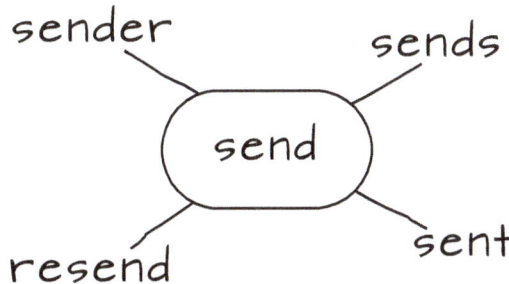

Day 3: Small group work on segmenting and writing words with the spelling pattern

Re-read the word list. Then put it out of sight and say, "We are going to practise listening to the sounds and remembering how they are spelt."

Choose three to five words from the list to work with. Ask students to:

- count the sounds in these words (they can use 'spelling fingers')
- draw Elkonin boxes for the words – one box for each sound

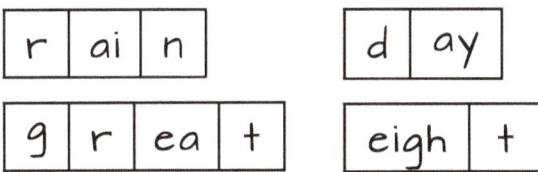

- move their fingers into the boxes as they segment each word again
- record the spelling patterns in the boxes
- rub out each word in the boxes and re-write it from memory.

Follow-up: Students create a word find for a friend.

continued ...

2. TRANSCRIPTION SKILLS

> **Day 4: Small group work on segmenting and spelling 'heart words'***
>
> Focus on irregular high-frequency words that were not included in the week's spelling pattern list.
>
> This routine is similar to Day 3, with one exception: before students have a go at rewriting the words from memory, as a group discuss the tricky or surprising 'heart parts'. For example, for students who have not yet learnt about the *wa* group, you could practise the word *was* and talk about the surprising *a* in the middle.
>
> * Heart words are high-frequency words with irregular spellings. For example, *they* has an irregular pattern of representing the 'long a' sound as *ey*. See our *Spelling made simple* programme (next page) for suggested heart words (and temporary heart words) at the end of the first five spelling units.

> **Day 5: Dictation**
>
> Re-read the word list. Then put it out of sight and say, "We are going to practise listening to the words in a sentence and remembering how they are spelt."
>
> - Choose a dictated sentence (or sentences) that will challenge students to apply the spelling pattern they have worked on during the week, or in previous weeks.
> - Read the dictation three times: first, at a natural pace; then slowly, two words at a time; and finally, at a natural pace again. Prompt students to listen for the sounds and to think of the patterns they know. Prompt them to listen for the end of each sentence and to use a full stop.
> - Display the sentence on the board so that students can mark their own work. Allocate ticks for particular knowledge items (including some that every student will achieve) – for example, "Give yourself a tick if you started the sentence with a capital letter."

Note: Thanks to Joy Allcock for the basis for the activity.

Assessment

When selecting assessment tools, consider your purpose.

Formative assessment tools. To identify learning needs and plan future lessons, use the assessment checkpoints provided in our *Spelling made simple* programme. Another tool that will support you to analyse students' errors and identify gaps in knowledge is Brann's analysis grid for spelling, for which you take the first 10 errors in a writing sample and consider whether these demonstrate difficulty with phonemic awareness (they may have sounds missing or added) or a lack of knowledge of spelling patterns and rules. Other options include:

- the Words Their Way series of real word tests, with a marking schedule that supports teachers to identify knowledge gaps
- a pseudoword test such as the one from Allcock (2008), which will show you which sound–letter patterns the students know, with information not confounded by words already memorised.

Summative assessment tools. To gain some insight into how your students are performing compared to their same-age peers, use a well-established standardised tool such as the Schonell, Hodder or the Morrison-McCall Spelling Scale.

2. TRANSCRIPTION SKILLS

Spelling programme: *Spelling made simple*

Follow this programme to support your students to learn more about spelling patterns and rules. Select one knowledge item a week to learn with your students. You'll soon feel quite confident teaching the code.

This resource has been developed in line with empirical research in the teaching of spelling (see, eg, Joshi et al 2008; Kilpatrick 2016). Key areas of knowledge and skill have been grouped together in the following units to simplify the processes of assessment, planning and teaching.

Before you begin the units (summarised in the overview below), administer our **Phonological awareness quick skills check** (on the next page) to junior students or to any older students who are demonstrating difficulty. This allows you to check that students are able to segment and blend words, swap sounds in words, and clap syllables. Note any students who need extra help in any of these areas.

Overview of this Spelling made simple *programme*

Unit	Focus	Page
1	Short vowels; single consonants; early digraphs (*ch, sh, th, ng*); early open syllable words	23
2	Other digraphs, including split digraphs; the trigraph *tch*; the floss rule	25
3	Long vowel sounds for *a, e* and *o; oo* as in *took*; the schwa endings *le/al* and *er/or*	27
4	Early suffixes (*ing, ed*); words ending in *y*; plurals	29
5	*r*-controlled and other vowels; the *all* chunk; *a* as /u/	32
6	Common prefixes and suffixes	34
7	The *wa/qua* group; 'long i' spelt *igh*; other vowels and the quadgraphs *augh/ough*	36
8	Contractions and homonyms for *they're, we're, you're*; the possessive apostrophe	38

We suggest taking the following approach to teaching each unit:

- To assess spelling knowledge, use the **Checkpoint** at the start of each of unit, either as a spelling test or as a guide to follow when you are analysing spelling attempts in students' draft writing books. Highlight the known items for each student and list their name on the checkpoint sheet under any knowledge items that you need to teach as next steps.
- Teach the knowledge gaps in each unit using the **Teaching guide**.

You could teach the units to a whole class for 10–15 minutes a day. If you choose to do this, be sure to teach to the stage of your lowest-achieving spellers during this time. Extend more advanced spellers by linking spelling and decoding during small group reading lessons. Then reinforce spelling knowledge during writing time.

2. TRANSCRIPTION SKILLS

Initial assessment: Phonological awareness quick skills check

Skills	Test item
Hearing syllables Say, "Our words have beats. They are called syllables. Watch me clap the beats in *spider*." (2 claps)	Clap the beats in: 1. *monkey* (2 beats) 2. *kangaroo* (3 beats) 3. *dog* (1 beat).
Student names:	
Segmenting Say, "Now we will listen to all the little sounds in words. We can count the sounds on our fingers. Like this: *cat, c-a-t*." (Show 3 spelling fingers).	Use your spelling fingers to count the sounds in: 4. *frog* (*f-r-o-g*, 4 sounds) 5. *fish* (*f-i-sh*, 3 sounds) 6. *bat* (*b-a-t*, 3 sounds).
Student names:	
Blending Say, "This is a guessing game. I'll make the sounds and you put them together to tell me the animal I'm thinking of. Like this: *sh-ar-k, shark*."	Tell me the animal: 7. *b-ir-d* (3 sounds) 8. *sh-ee-p* (3 sounds) 9. *c-r-a-b* (4 sounds).
Student names:	
Hearing beginning, middle, and end sounds Say: • "The first sound in *rat* is [/r/ sound]. What is the first sound in *goat*?" • "The last sound in *worm* is [/m/ sound]. What is the last sound in *hen*?" • "The middle sound in *pig* is ['short i' sound]. What is the middle sound in *hen*?" Note: Refer to and make the **sounds** – not letter names.	Tell me the target sound in: 10. *goat* (first sound /g/) 11. *hen* (last sound /n/) 12. *rat* (middle sound 'short a').
Student names:	
Sound swapping This final task is only for students who have scored at least 10 for the first 12 items, and who have sound–letter knowledge and formation for short vowels and single consonants. You will need a whiteboard and marker. • Record *pig* on the whiteboard. Say, "We will do a magic trick on the word. This says *pig*. Can you change it to *big*? What letter will you rub out? What will you write instead?" • Repeat to change *big* to *bit*, and *bit* to *bat*.	Change: 13. *pig* to *big* 14. *big* to *bit* 15. *bit* to *bat*.
Student names:	

2. TRANSCRIPTION SKILLS

Unit 1: Short vowels; single consonants; early digraphs (*ch, sh, th, ng*); early open syllable words

Unit 1: Checkpoint

Word	Short vowels	Single consonants (not all sounds are tested)	First digraphs	First open syllable words
van	a	v n		
hid	i	h d		
dog	o	d g		
leg	e	l g		
much	u	m	ch	
shop	o	p	sh	
then	e	n	th (voiced)	
sing	i	s	ng	
with	i	w	th (unvoiced)	
he				e
go				o
Student names for teaching				

2. TRANSCRIPTION SKILLS

Unit 1: Teaching guide – short vowels; single consonants; early digraphs (ch, sh, th, ng); early open syllable words

Teaching sequence	Spelling pattern	Explanation	Examples
Teach these single-letter sounds over the first 10–20 weeks at school. Interchange your teaching of vowels and consonants. Follow the same scope and sequence as for reading. Teach four a week, providing opportunities for revision.	Short vowels	These sounds are made with an open mouth. The short vowel syllable is the most common syllable type.	Teach these using toys with initial sounds (*apple, ant, egg, insect, orange, umbrella*) and CVC words (*cat, hat, van, peg, leg, bed, lid, pig, pot, fish, frog, dog, cup, cub, jug*).
	Single consonant sounds	Teach the hard c /k/ sound in this unit, and the hard g /g/. These are the most common sounds for these letters.	CVC words are good for teaching these too as it is easier for five-year-olds to segment shorter words. Use some other toys/words too. Find examples with sounds at the beginning, middle and end of words. For example, for *b*: *ball, robot, cub*.
Teach these after the single-letter sounds. Move at a slower pace to avoid confusion. Teach two a week.	sh	Two letters, one sound.	*ship, shop, cash, shell, fish, posh*
	ch	Two letters, one sound.	*chop, chips, champ, chick, much, such*
	th	There are two *th* sounds: unvoiced and voiced.	Unvoiced: *three, thermometer, cloth, moth, stethoscope, teeth, bath* Voiced: *feather, mother, father, brother, the, then, that, they*
	ng	The *ng* never occurs at the beginning of a word.	*song, string, wing, ring, stingray*
Heart words: *I, the, to, a, my, was, are*			

2. TRANSCRIPTION SKILLS

Unit 2: Other digraphs, including split digraphs; the trigraph *tch*; the floss rule

Unit 2: Checkpoint

Word	Digraphs	The trigraph *tch*	Split digraph for long vowels	Floss rule
when	wh			
phone	ph		o_e	
quick	qu ck			
match		tch		
bike			i_e	
cake			a_e	
will				ll
miss				ss
puff				ff
Student names for teaching				

Unit 2: Teaching guide – other digraphs, including split digraphs; the trigraph tch; *the floss rule*

Teaching sequence	Pattern or rule	Explanation	Examples
Week 1	Open and closed syllables	Closed syllables contain a short vowel and end with a consonant. They are the most common syllable type. Open syllables end with a long vowel sound. Discuss the rules for closed and open syllables. Using one-syllable words, teach your students to practise hearing whether a syllable is closed or open.	Closed: *cat, sit, box, mat, dog, frog, hand, mum, dad, truck, jet, fish, with, that, much, then* Open: *day, way, say, hi, go, me, see, to, my, by*
	Early, open syllable words	A number of early high-frequency words are in this group.	*he, me, we, be, she, go*
Week 2	wh	*wh* usually makes the /w/ sound. (An obvious exception is the word *who*, which you should not teach as part of this unit.)	*when, where, what, why, wheel, white, while*
	ph	Words with *ph* have Greek origins. The Greek alphabet has a letter 'phi' which sounds like /f/.	*phone, photo, phonics, phantom, alphabet, dolphin, elephant, trophy, orphan, phantom*

continued ...

© Essential Resources Educational Publishers Ltd

2. TRANSCRIPTION SKILLS

Teaching sequence	Pattern or rule	Explanation	Examples
Week 3	qu	*q* is always followed by *u*.	*queen, quick, quiet, quilt, question, equal, squid*
	ck	*ck* comes at the end of single syllable words with short vowel sounds – to spell /k/. It comes at the end of short vowel syllables with suffixes (*flicked, shocking, trucker*). It does not come after long vowel sounds (*beak*) or other vowel sounds (*park*). It does not come after short vowels in multisyllable words (*picnic*), unless they are compound words (*backpack*).	*sack, pack, rack, back, deck, neck, peck, pick, sick, flick, tick, kick, rock, sock, shock, block, lock, duck, luck, suck, muck, truck*
Week 4	The trigraph tch	*tch* is a trigraph – meaning that three letters represent one sound. *tch* represents the same sound as *ch* (as in *lunch*). It is used at the ends of words, directly following the vowel (compare *lunch* and *latch*).	*match, witch, catch, glitch, fetch, latch*
Week 5	Split digraph	The split digraph pattern is *a_e, e_e, i_e, o_e* or *u_e*. The first consonant and the *e* together make the first vowel long (it 'says its own name'). For example, *hop* changes to *hope, mad* changes to *made*. This is a useful rule to know early as many common words are spelt in this way.	*made, make, lake, take, bake, cake, shake, shape, like, bike, hike, kite, hope, poke, spoke, rope*
Week 6	Floss rule	When a short-vowel, one-syllable word ends in *f, l, s* or *z*, double the final consonant.	*off, puff, will, still, miss, loss, boss, mess, less, buzz, jazz*
Heart words: *come, some, here, said, you, your*			

A note about blends

At about this stage of development, some reading sequences call for the teaching of *s, l, r* and end blends. However, a blend is two distinct sounds. Therefore, if we teach word segmentation well, students will be able to hear, articulate and spell all blends without explicit teaching of the 'blended' unit.

However, certain blends can be tricky to hear, so you may need to provide students with extra support. Explain that the sounds come close together and that one sound can be slightly changed because of the sound that comes before or after. Talk about the different positions of your tongue, teeth and lips as you articulate the sounds.

- The blend *dr* (*drink*) can sound like /j/.
- The blend *st* (*stop*) can sound like 'sd', though no English words start with *sd*.
- The blend *sp* (*spin*) can sound like 'sb', though no English words start with *sb*.
- The blend *tr* (*truck*) can sound like 'ch'.

2. TRANSCRIPTION SKILLS

Unit 3: Long vowel sounds for *a, e* and *o; oo* as in *took*; the schwa endings *le/al* and *er/or*

Unit 3: Checkpoint

Word	'Long a' – ai	'Long a' – ay	'Long e' – ea	'Long e' – ee	'Long o' – oa	'Long o' – ow	oo	u	Schwa er/or	Schwa le/al
rain	ai									
took							oo			
seen				ee						
day		ay								
boat					oa					
bow						ow				
beach			ea							
bush								u		
doctor									or	
brittle										le
sister									er	
metal										al
Student names for teaching										

Unit 3: Teaching guide – long vowel sounds for a, e and o; oo *as in* took; *the* schwa *endings* le/al *and* er/or

Teaching sequence	Pattern or rule	Explanation	Examples
Week 1	'Long a' – ai	This pattern occurs in the middle of a syllable.	*rain, pain, train, drain, afraid, raid, paid, braid, main, sail*
Week 2	'Long a' – ay	This pattern occurs at the end of a syllable.	*day, say, may, way, pay, stay, away, today, crayon, daytime, layer*
Week 3	'Long e' – ea	There is no rule for when to use *ea*, *ee* or just *e*. You could discuss homonyms (words that sound the same but have different meanings) while teaching these patterns: *sea/see*; *meat/meet*. *Mean* has several different meanings but is always spelt the same.	*beach, peach, tea, sea, eat, teach, meat, steam, mean, leap, beneath, treaty, creature*
Week 4	'Long e' – ee		*feet, meet, free, see, weed, deep, sweet, bleed, breeze, speech, between, thirteen, fourteen, referee*

continued ...

2. TRANSCRIPTION SKILLS

Teaching sequence	Pattern or rule	Explanation	Examples
Week 5	'Long o' – *oa*	The *oa* and *ow* spellings are used for the long *o* sound in the middle of a syllable, whereas just *o* and *oe* spellings are used at the end.	*goat, boat, soak, float, roast, coat, soap, toast, groan, throat*
Week 6	'Long o' – *ow*	You could discuss homonyms *know* and *no*. The *kn* spelling comes from words of Germanic origin, adopted into Old English. The *k* was originally pronounced in English but became silent in the 17th or 18th century. Other spellings for the 'long o' are *o* (*go, so*) and *oe* (*toe, hoe, woe*).	*bow, row, low, own, tow, blow, flow, glow, know, show, slow, snow, follow, hollow, window*
Week 7	*oo* as in *took*	There is no rule for when to use *oo* or *u*.	*took, book, look, shook, foot, cook, hook, good, stood, hood, wood*
Week 8	*u* as in *put*		*put, push, pull, bush, bull, full*
Week 9	Schwa endings *er* and *or*	The schwa is the vowel sound in an unstressed syllable, made when the tongue, lips and jaw are relaxed. The schwa suffixes (word endings) *er* and *or* often appear in nouns and 'nouns of action' (meaning a person or thing that does something, eg, *hunter, teacher, doctor*). The *er* ending also appears in prepositions (eg, *after*) and conjunctions (eg, *however*). The *er* ending is more common than the *or* ending.	*sister, brother, mother, father, computer, flower, ladder, finger, weather, teacher, dinner, number, builder, farmer, hunter, after, however, forever* *doctor, investigator, actor, director, survivor, inspector, visitor, author, ancestor, tractor*
Week 10	Schwa *le* and *al*	The schwa sound occurs in many different syllables (and has a range of spellings). Words with the *le* schwa suffix come from Old English. These words were originally spelt *el* but the spelling has changed over time. Many words with *le* describe a repeated action (eg, *sparkle*). The *al* suffix is found in nouns (eg, *animal*). It can create adjectives that describe a likeness – named by the stem or root of the word (eg, with the stem *music*, the adjective *musical*).	*little, battle, double, bangle, beetle, buckle, crumble, fiddle, gamble, grumble, handle, nibble, riddle, rumble, sparkle* *criminal, tropical, mythical, total, loyal, usual, spiral, mammal, animal, equal, musical, crystal, natural, hospital*

Heart words: *one, once, have, give, live, there, where, two, too*

2. TRANSCRIPTION SKILLS

Unit 4: Early suffixes (*ing, ed*); words ending in *y*; plurals
Unit 4: Checkpoint

Word	Suffix *ed*	Suffix *ing*	Double the middle consonant when adding *ed* to a short vowel syllable	Double the middle consonant when adding *ing* to a short vowel syllable	Take away the final *e* when adding *ing*	Words ending in *y*	Plurals of words ending in *y*	Plurals with *s* or *es*	The soft *c* and *g* before *e, i* or *y**
running		ing		nn					
mopped	ed		pp						
baby						y			
babies							ies		
hoping					hoping				
age									g
fly						y			
icy									c
hands								s	
boxes								es	
Student names for teaching									

*Not all patterns are assessed here. We often pronounce *c* as /s/ and *g* as /j/ when either of these letters is followed by *e, i* or *y*.

2. TRANSCRIPTION SKILLS

Unit 4: Teaching guide – early suffixes (ing, ed); words ending in y; plurals

Teaching sequence	Pattern or rule	Explanation	Examples
Week 1	Exploring *ing* and *ed* Double the middle consonant when adding *ing* or *ed* to short vowel/ closed syllables	Doubling the middle consonant 'protects' the short vowel (and keeps it short). Consider the different pronunciations of *hopping, hopped, hoping, hoped*. For short vowel syllables that already end with two consonants, we do not double either consonant. The *ing* makes the present form of the verb. It describes an action happening now (eg, *I am running*). The *ing* also appears at the end of some nouns (eg, *ceiling, building*). The *ed* makes the past form of the verb. It describes an action that has already happened (eg, *the car stopped*). Some verbs do not take *ed* to form the past participle. These words change in different ways (eg, *sit, sat*). Remember that *ing* consists of two sounds: 'i-ng'. Similar 'chunks' (or rime units) can be made by substituting the vowel (think of *bang, song, flung*). Remember that with *ed*, we do not hear a sound for *e*. This suffix sounds like part of a consonant cluster on the end of a word (eg, say *stopped*).	*hop, hopping, hopped* *stop, stopping, stopped* *mop, mopping, mopped* *hug, hugging, hugged* *pat, patting, patted* *dig, digging, dug* *sit, sitting, sat* *run, running, ran* *swim, swimming, swam* *get, getting, got* *jump, jumping, jumped* *smash, smashing, smashed* *crash, crashing, crashed* *shop, shopping, shopped* *lift, lifting, lifted* *brush, brushing, brushed* *singing, singing, sang* *think, thinking, thought*
Week 2	Adding *ing* and *ed* to other syllables types	Syllables with long vowel digraphs (vowel teams) – *ai, ay, ea, ee, oa, ow, oo* – do not change before adding *ing* or *ed*. Some change form for past tense instead of adding *ed* (eg, *bleed, bleeding, bled*). We hear a schwa sound when pronouncing the *ed* suffix at the end of a word that begins with a 'long e' or 'long o' syllable (eg, *floated*). Some *oo* words (eg, *took, shook*) are past tense forms of their root word (*take, shake*). Learn how to add endings to words with *e* endings in Week 3 of this unit.	*rain, raining, rained* *train, training, trained* *drain, draining, drained* *stay, staying, stayed* *play, playing, played* *weed, weeding, weeded* *bleed, bleeding, bled* *keep, keeping, kept* *meet, meeting, met* *see, seeing, seen* *eat, eating, ate* *leap, leaping, leapt* *float, floating, floated* *roast, roasting, roasted* *boast, boasting, boasted* *tow, towing, towed* *row, rowing, rowed* *look, looking, looked* *cook, cooking, cooked*

continued ...

2. TRANSCRIPTION SKILLS

Teaching sequence	Pattern or rule	Explanation	Examples
Week 3	Taking away the final *e* when adding *ing*	This rule is simple: take away the final *e* before adding *ing*. Begin the week with some revision of the split digraph long vowel spelling pattern (covered in Unit 2).	*make, making; take, taking; bake, baking; fade, fading; shade, shading; graze, grazing; shake, shaking; rise, rising; dive, diving; poke, poking; hope, hoping; code, coding; use, using; fuse, fusing*
Week 4	Words ending in *y*	At the end of words with one syllable, *y* usually represents the sound of the 'long i'. At the end of words with two or more syllables, *y* usually represents the sound of the 'long e'. The one-syllable word *key* and some two-syllable words use *ey* together, representing the 'long e'. The *ay* ending represents the 'long a' sound. The *oy*, as in *toy*, represents a different vowel sound. This ending is found in one- and two-syllable words.	One syllable: *my, by, fly, try, sky, shy, sly, fry, cry, dry* Two syllables: *funny, happy, lazy, sunny, jelly, bunny, sticky, shiny, sleepy, party, puppy, berry* The *ey*: *money, honey, monkey, key* The *ay*: *day, way, say, today, mayday, away* The *oy*: *boy, toy, joy, decoy*
Week 5	Plurals of words ending in *y*	For most words ending in *y*, take off the *y* and add *ies*. For most words ending in a vowel + *y*, just add *s*.	*baby, babies; fly, flies; berry, berries; bunny, bunnies; spy, spies; party, parties; puppy, puppies* *day, days; play, plays; monkey, monkeys; boy, boys; toy, toys*
Week 6	Plurals of other words: *s* or *es*	Add *s* to most other words to make them plural. But if the word ends in *s, ss, z, ch* or *sh*, add *es*.	Add *s*: *train, trains; doll, dolls; car, cars; pencil, pencils; kid, kids; apple, apples; shark, sharks* Add *es*: *bus, buses; kiss, kisses; quiz, quizzes; church, churches; fish, fishes*
Week 7	The soft *c* and *g* before *e, i* or *y*	When *c* or *g* comes before *e, i* or *y*, the sound is soft: /s/ or /j/. But for words ending with *ggy*, the *gg* represents a hard /g/ sound (eg, *doggy, baggy, soggy, foggy*).	Soft *c*: *nice, price, mice, race, centre, cinder, cinema, recycle, lacy* Soft *g*: *ginger, gin, giant, gentleman, gesture, generous, huge, age, agent, gym, gypsy, technology, strategy, energy, ecology, stingy*
Heart words: *talk, walk, would, should, could, who*			

2. TRANSCRIPTION SKILLS

Unit 5: *r*-controlled and other vowels; the *all* chunk; *a* as /u/

Unit 5: Checkpoint

Words	*r*-controlled vowels	*ou/ow*	*oy/oi*	the chunk *all*	*a* as /u/
curly	ur				
boy			oy		
town		ow			
shirt	ir				
mouth		ou			
smart	ar				
port	or				
soil			oi		
tall				all	
away					a
Student names for teaching					

Unit 5: Teaching guide – r-controlled and other vowels; the *all* chunk; *a* as /u/

Teaching sequence	Pattern or rule	Explanation	Examples
Week 1	*r*-controlled vowels: *ar, or* sounds	When a vowel is followed by *r* in the middle of a word, it represents a different vowel sound from the ones covered so far. These new sounds are **r-controlled vowels**. The *ar* chunk always represents the same sound (eg, *farm*). The *or* chunk always represents the same sound (eg, *corn*). Remember that *or* and *er* at the end of a word make the schwa sound (see Unit 3).	The *ar*: *car, arm, far, bar, jar, star, scar, start, barn, bark, dart, yard, farm, smart, garden, marbles, art, mark, dark, carpet, part* The *or*: *corn, born, or, fork, short, morning, snore, horn, form, north, force, for, sort, shore, pork, torch, before, forget*

continued …

2. TRANSCRIPTION SKILLS

Teaching sequence	Pattern or rule	Explanation	Examples
Week 2	*r*-controlled vowels: 'er' sound	The letters *er, ir* or *ur* can represent the 'er' sound. For example, *fern, shirt* and *curl* all have the same vowel sound but each is spelt differently. Occasionally *or* can represent the 'er' sound (eg, *word*).	The *er*: *her, term, germ, nerve, alert, person, perfume, herbs, jerky* The *ir*: *bird, shirt, skirt, first, third, circus, girl, twirl, stir, squirm, dirt, sir, chirp, dirty, thirsty, circle, birthday* The *ur*: *curl, fur, blur, turtle, burn, curse, burst, turn, purse, nurse, hurt, burp, Thursday, purple, church*
Week 3	*ou* and *ow*	The 'ou' sound (as in *out*) can be represented by *ou* and *ow*. This sound is not long or short; it is something different. No consistent rule applies for which spelling to use. But the *ou* pattern never occurs at the end of a word, whereas the *ow* pattern sometimes does.	The *ou*: *out, our, ouch, outside, couch, shout, pouch, house, mouse, count, found, sound, round, bounce, cloud, south, mountain* The *ow*: *cow, how, now, brow, vow, owl, down, town, frown, tower, power, towel, vowel, growl, frown, drown*
Week 4	*oy* and *oi*	Either *oi* or *oy* can represent the 'oi' sound. This sound is not long or short; it is something different. This sound is an easy-to-hear diphthong. That is, it starts as one sound and moves towards the other (listen to this effect in *boil* and *toy*). Both spelling patterns occur occasionally at the beginning of a word. When the sound comes at the start of or in the middle of a syllable, use *oi*. When it comes at the end of a syllable or word, use *oy*.	The *oi*: *ointment, join, coin, boil, foil, soil, spoil, point, poison, oink, toilet, voice, noise, choice, moist, noisy, avoid* The *oy*: *oyster, toy, soy, boy, destroy, annoy, employ, enjoy, royal, loyal, foyer, voyage*
Week 6	The pattern *all*	The *all* spelling pattern appears in many common words. As a word, *all* means the whole of something. The prefix *al* also means the whole of something (eg, in *always*). A prefix is a word part that comes in front of the root word to change its meaning.	The pattern *all*: *all, small, ball, call, wall, hall, tall, call, install, fall* The prefix *al*: *almost, always, almighty, altogether, also, although*
Week 7	*a* as /u/	When the letter a has a syllable to itself, it usually represents the sound /u/.	*a, away, another, again, ago, apart, across, cola, sofa, mama, papa*
Heart words: *because, please, only, four, eight, warm, laugh, shall*			

© Essential Resources Educational Publishers Ltd

2. TRANSCRIPTION SKILLS

Unit 6: Common prefixes and suffixes

Unit 6: Checkpoint

Words	Suffix *est*	Suffix *less*	Suffix *ful*	Suffix *tion*	Prefix *dis*	Prefix *re*	Prefix *in*	Prefix *un*	Changing *y* to *i*
loveliest	est								i
useless		less							
playful			ful						
lotion				tion					
dislike					dis				
remain						re			
inject							in		
undo								un	
Student names for teaching									

Note: The words in this group may be easy to spell but working on the meanings of these prefixes is another valid activity. Consider using this as a check for understanding rather than spelling.

Unit 6: Teaching guide – common prefixes and suffixes

Teaching sequence	Pattern or rule	Explanation	Examples
Week 1	What is a suffix? What is a rime unit? The suffix *est*	A **suffix** is a word part that is added to the end of a root word and changes its meaning. A **rime unit** is the string of letters that follow the first consonant in a syllable. The *est* suffix creates words that describe the greatest or most extreme form of something (eg, *long, longest*). It is added to adjectives and adverbs (words that describe). As a suffix, *est* has the schwa as its vowel sound (see Unit 3). To add *est* to a word ending in *y*, change the *y* to *i* (eg, *happy, happiest*). To add *est* to a closed (short vowel) syllable, double the final consonant (eg, *big, biggest*). It also appears as a rime unit in other parts of words (eg, in *best, estimate*).	Suffix *est*: *biggest, fattest, loudest, smallest, fastest, slowest, longest, shortest, happiest, loveliest, angriest, hungriest* Rime unit *est*: *best, rest, nest, pest, festive, crest, test, quest, chest, west, estimate, estate*
Week 2	The suffix *less*	The suffix *less* means without. It is added to nouns (eg, *child, childless*). The vowel sound is the schwa.	*nameless, homeless, childless, friendless, spotless, heartless, breathless, painless, hopeless, useless, meaningless*

continued …

2. TRANSCRIPTION SKILLS

Teaching sequence	Pattern or rule	Explanation	Examples
Week 3	The suffix *ful*	The suffix *ful* means full of something. It is added to nouns. To add *ful* to words that end in *y*, change the *y* to *i* (*beauty, beautiful*).	*helpful, painful, wonderful, thankful, respectful, beautiful, hurtful, harmful, successful, skilful, delightful*
Week 4	The suffix *tion*	The suffix *tion* changes a verb (an action word) to a noun (a naming word) (eg, *create, creation*). Show the difference between the role of the verb and the noun in the context of sentences (eg, *I create art.* vs *Look at my creation.*) To add *tion* to a word with a silent *e*, take away the *e* (eg, *create, creation*). A suffix that looks and sounds similar is *sion* (eg, *invasion, decision, explosion*). Compare the sounds of *vision* and *potion* to help students decide which spelling to use.	*act, action; create, creation; collect, collection; infect, infection; elect, election; invent, invention; introduce, introduction; communicate, communication* Other nouns do not have a verb form or look very different from their verb form: *lotion, commotion, potion, motion, option, nation, extinction, evolution*
Week 5	What is a prefix? The prefix *dis*	A prefix is a word part that is added to the beginning of a root word. It has a meaning of its own and changes the meaning of the root word. The prefix *dis* can reverse the meaning of the root word (eg, *ability, disability*).	*ability, disability; arm, disarm; like, dislike; content, discontent; appear, disappear; own, disown; agree, disagree; infect, disinfect; honest, dishonest; order, disorder* Words with a less obvious relationship with the root: *discover, disgrace, disguise*
Week 6	The prefix *re*	The **prefix** *re* can mean again (eg, in *recycle*). It can mean backward or withdrawal (eg, in *revert, reverse*). Some root words begin with *re* or have the prefix *re* with a less obvious relationship with the root.	Meaning again: *rebuild, redo, reheat, replay, recycle, rediscover, remarry, rearrange, review* Meaning backward: *reverie, reverse* Other words: *reaction, result, remain, reduce, region, relax, respect, record, recover*
Week 7	The prefix *in*	The prefix *in* usually means not (eg, *insane*). It can also mean in or into (eg, *inject*).	*inject, influx, insane, independent, invalid, insecure, inactive, incomplete, inappropriate, incorrect, inconvenient, invisible, informal*
Week 8	The prefix *un*	The prefix *un* almost always means not (eg, *unclean*). When attached to a verb, it often means the 'not' state has been changed in some way (eg, *undone*).	*unclean, undone, unusual, unripe, unhappy, untidy, undress, untie, unwell, untrue, unfinished, uncertain*

© Essential Resources Educational Publishers Ltd

2. TRANSCRIPTION SKILLS

Unit 7: The *wa/qua* group; 'long i' spelt *igh*; other vowels and the quadgraphs *augh/ough*

Unit 7: checkpoint

Words	augh/ough	wa/qua group	'Long i' – igh	ew/ue/ui	au/aw
caught	augh				
want		wa			
bought	ough				
light			igh		
flew				ew	
quad		qua			
clue				ue	
automatic					au
suit				ui	
awful					aw
Student names for teaching					

Unit 7: Teaching guide – the wa/qua *group; 'long i' spelt* igh*; other vowels and the quadgraphs* augh/ough

Teaching sequence	Pattern or rule	Explanation	Examples
Week 1	The 'long i' *igh*	The 'long i' we hear can be spelt *igh*. This *igh* is a trigraph, meaning it consists of three letters making one sound. This unusual-looking spelling originally came from German words, adopted into Old English. In Unit 2, students learnt how to spell the 'long i' with a split digraph (eg, in *like*). Another common 'long i' spelling is *ie* (eg, *pie, flies, tries, tie, lie*). All of these 'long i' spellings can occur in the middle of syllables and words.	*night, sight, bright, fight, sight, flight*

continued ...

2. TRANSCRIPTION SKILLS

Teaching sequence	Pattern or rule	Explanation	Examples
Week 2	au, aw	The *au* and *aw* patterns or vowel teams can represent the sound 'or'. Either spelling can occur at the beginning or in the middle of a word. The *aw* spelling can occur at the end of a word too.	The *au*: August, audio, automatic, author, autumn, astronaut, cause, pause, laundry, exhaust, haunt, sauce, saucer The *aw*: awe, law, awful, draw, claw, raw, dawn, fawn, saw, squawk, crawl, scrawl, yawn, straw
Week 3	augh, ough	The *augh* and *ough* patterns are quadgraphs, meaning that four letters make one sound. When teaching the *ough* group, spend some time discussing the single sound letter difference between and the different meanings of *bought* and *brought*. Work into these words from the sound *or*. But remember that the *ough* and *augh* can represent other sounds too (eg, *ough* as in *through, drought, cough*; *augh* as in *laugh*). These unusual-looking spellings originally came from German words, adopted into Old English.	The *ough*: thought, fought, brought, bought, thoughtful, sought The *augh*: daughter, caught, taught, naughty
Week 4	The *wa, qua* group	The 'short o' sound we hear after *w* or *qu* is spelt with an *a*.	was, watch, want, what, wash, wallet, swap, swan, quantity, quad, quality, squash
Week 5	ue, ew, ui	The patterns *ue, ew* and *ui* can all occur in the middle or at the end of a syllable or word. There is no rule to tell us which to use when. The *ew* spelling occurs at the beginning of *ewe* and *ewer*. When teaching *ew*, discuss the different spellings and meanings of the homonyms *new–knew*.	The *ue*: glue, clue, rescue, tissue, argue, true, blue The *ew*: flew, new, knew, grew, dew, chew, crew, newspaper, stew, ewe The *ui*: fruit, juice, cruise, suit, bruise, recruit, ruined

2. TRANSCRIPTION SKILLS

Unit 8: Contractions and homonyms for *they're, we're, you're*; the possessive apostrophe

Unit 8: Checkpoint

Words	Contractions	*their/there/they're*	*you/you're*	*where/we're/were*	Possessive apostrophe
I've	I've				
their*		their			
there*		there			
they're*		they're			
your*			your		
you're*			you're		
where*				where	
we're*				we're	
were*				were	
Mum's car					Mum's
Student names for teaching					

*Put these words into sentences when testing them.

2. TRANSCRIPTION SKILLS

Unit 8: Teaching guide – contractions and homonyms for they're, we're, you're; *the possessive apostrophe*

Teaching sequence	Pattern or rule	Explanation	Examples
Week 1	What is a contraction?	A **contraction** is a word made by putting two words together and taking out one or more letters. Add an apostrophe to show where the missing letters were.	*I have, I've; I will, I'll; do not, don't; cannot, can't; we are, we're; we will, we'll; did not, didn't; could not, couldn't; would not, wouldn't; should not, shouldn't; has not, hasn't; have not, haven't; they are, they're; we are, we're; you are, you're; that is, that's; it is, it's* A tricky example: *will not, won't*
Week 2	*there, their, they're*	*There, their* and *they're* are homonyms. They sound the same, but have different spellings and meanings. *There* can mean at that place. It can also introduce a fact or a thing. *Their* means belonging to them. *They're* is the contraction for *they are*.	The mountain is over *there*. *There* are lots of students in this school. *There* is a nice hotel on the corner. That's *their* house. *They're* a really nice group of friends.
Week 3	*your, you're*	*Your* and *you're* are homonyms. *Your* means belonging to you. *You're* is the contraction of *you are*.	I like *your* hat. *You're* really good at swimming.
Week 4	*where, we're, were*	*Where* and *we're* are homonyms, but *were* is pronounced differently. *Where* means a place or asks a question about a place. *We're* is the contraction of *we are*. *Were* is the past tense of the verb *to be*, used for the second person (*you*) and for plurals (*we, they*).	*Where* do you live? I like to go *where* it is warmest. *We're* tired from our walk. You *were* so kind to me.
Week 5	The possessive apostrophe	When something belongs to someone, show this by using *'s* after the noun/name for that someone. When something belongs to a group, use *'s* after the noun of that group. Even though *it* can be a pronoun for a non-human creature, never give it a possessive apostrophe. Only use an apostrophe in the contraction *it's* (from *it is*).	*Tama's* brother is a fast runner. (The brother belongs to Tama.) That is *Dad's* house. (The house belongs to Dad.) The *men's* toilets are over there. (The toilets are for the men.) The *children's* books are on the table. (The books belong to the children.) The dog ate *its* bone. (The dog belongs to the dog but *its* has no possessive apostrophe.)

Note: While this unit only covers a few words in some weeks, it helps to move slowly through this content as it is complex. To avoid confusion, provide simple explanations and remind students of these every day. Then model how to use the words and provide lots of practice examples for students to work on. Mark these 'on the spot' to check for understanding and give immediate feedback.

3. Translation

Translation means turning thoughts into sentences. It requires vocabulary knowledge and sentence-generation skills (Kent et al 2014). Oral practice is a great way to start as this will give students opportunities to grow their knowledge, without becoming overloaded by the demands of spelling and handwriting (Arfé et al 2021).

Teaching vocabulary

Vocabulary knowledge is essential to success with writing as it allows students to express their message precisely and creatively. It is central to reading development too: vocabulary knowledge is a strong predictor of reading comprehension by Year 5 and the main predictor by Year 8 (Biemiller 2012; Hoover and Gough 1990).

Significantly, the vocabulary size of high- and low-achieving students differs substantially, as it does between students from high- and low-income backgrounds. Biemiller (2012) reports that by the end of Year 3 (Grade 2), students in the highest achievement quartile know twice as many word meanings as those in the lowest quartile (about 8,000 compared with 4,000). Graves and colleagues (1982) estimate that in Year 1 (Grade 1), students with a high socioeconomic status (SES) know 50% more words than their low SES counterparts.

High-quality vocabulary instruction is therefore crucial. Without it, low-vocabulary students are likely to fall further behind – in literacy and in other curriculum areas. This is because, when listening and reading, a certain level of vocabulary knowledge is required to infer the meanings of any other new words (Pondiscio 2015; Tunmer and Chapman 2012). For example, to uncover the meaning of the word *fumerole* from the sentence, "A fumerole discharges water vapour caused by a hydrothermal system", students would first need to know the meanings of *discharges, vapour* and *hydrothermal*.

It is encouraging that, given appropriate instruction, students in all groups may learn new words at the same rate. Instruction should occur every day and should include opportunities for incidental learning of vocabulary – through immersion in mature speech and linguistically rich texts, as well as planned and explicit teaching of target words and word families.

In their meta-analysis of 67 preschool and kindergarten (Year 1) intervention studies, Marulis and Neuman (2010) revealed a strong overall effect size of 0.88. Whole-class teaching proved to be just as effective as small-group and one-on-one interventions; and short sessions (of 20 minutes or less) were just as effective as longer ones. In addition, students could make significant progress over a limited number of sessions (18 or fewer), especially when these programmes used targeted assessments and specific learning objectives. The greatest gains were made when researchers or qualified teachers delivered the training, while studies in which childcare providers and parents conducted training showed smaller effects.

Incidental learning

Evidently, much word learning occurs incidentally, as students are exposed to vocabulary both orally and in the context of reading (Nagy et al 1985). Teachers can strengthen this incidental learning in two ways.

First, we can model sophisticated language use in everyday contexts. For example, we might use it in referring to familiar classroom activities – "*Assemble* on the courts" – or to student behaviour – "Thomas showed *compassion*". We might use it while teaching across the curriculum too: "The universe is possibly *infinite*" (Lane and Allen, 2010). We can encourage students to do the same, perhaps by asking them to brainstorm common phrases and then recraft these using a thesaurus. Alternatively we might ask them to 'collect' words according to certain categories, such as emotive words, onomatopoeia or 'smart words'. We could then put their collected words into labelled jars and draw them out to discuss during transitions between lessons (Wilfong 2021).

Second, we can teach students how to use context cues to uncover word meanings while they read independently. For this, we must explicitly teach the process, using modelling (thinking aloud about the word and its meaning) and guided practice. Further, we must show students the specific types of cues authors use. In general, authors may explain word meanings directly (eg, "*Solar energy* is energy derived from the sun's rays"), or use synonyms as cues – that is, words and phrases with a similar meaning – alongside the target word (eg, "the pain *persisted*, keeping him awake throughout the night"). Prompt students to reflect on the author's use of a particular cue, by asking questions such as, "Can you see how the author uses a synonym cue to help you figure out the word?" Teach students to use these types of cues in their own writing too (Wilfong 2021).

Selecting words for teaching

While much vocabulary learning will occur incidentally, this kind of learning is not enough to fully address the difficulties of struggling readers. Explicit instruction in word meanings is essential.

You should consider vocabulary challenges at the outset of a unit of work or before reading with students. Consider which words to teach using explicit instruction. You might select these target words in a number of ways, such as the following.

Beck and colleagues (2013) recommend using a three-tiered system to select words:
- Tier One words are common, everyday words that are typically used in oral language.
- Tier Two words are more wide-ranging and specific. They are used more often in written language than in conversation (eg, *emerge*).
- Tier Three are domain specific (eg, *enzyme*) and may be rarely used.

These researchers suggest that Tier Two words are best suited for vocabulary instruction because students are less likely to encounter them in conversation and knowing them will help students to access written text. (Note that students will also encounter and study Tier Three words as they work across other curriculum areas, provided that lessons are 'knowledge rich'.) In particular, choose Tier Two words that are useful and important, that express already familiar concepts in a more sophisticated way and that offer a variety of uses to explore (eg, students might use *establish* in the context of establishing a business or reputation, or to confirm the truth of something). Be aware that verbally defined or abstract words (eg, *jealousy*) may be more important to teach than those with concrete meanings (eg, *propeller*).

Biemiller (2012) tested students at different levels using Dale and O'Rourke's Living Word Vocabulary. His results suggest that word learning follows a sequence, such that students learn certain words earlier and others later. As a result also, students with a relatively small vocabulary know the meanings of the earlier words, while those with larger vocabularies know these early words plus others. From this work, Biemiller developed a list of words for instruction, including 1,600 words by the end of Year 3 (Grade 2) and a further 2,900 words by the end of Year 7 (Grade 6). You can access these lists in Biemiller's (2009) monograph Words Worth Teaching. Alternatively use Averil Coxhead's Academic Word List of 570 root words and 3,000 derived meanings (**www.uefap.com/vocab/select/awl.htm**), which she developed in a similar way to Biemiller's list, and many of the words overlap.

3. TRANSLATION

Classroom routines for explicit teaching of vocabulary knowledge

What does it mean to know a word? Being able to pronounce it correctly, produce it in written form and understand its meaning are priorities for young learners, but the following aspects are also important to cover in your teaching:

- For students to **identify meaningful word parts**, explicitly teach Greek and Latin roots, which are present in 60% of multisyllabic words. Understanding a single root can help a student to uncover the meanings of up to 20 words (Wilfong 2021). Teaching affixes (prefixes and suffixes) will further support this learning. Begin with the most common roots and affixes (see Table 2 in Chapter 2). Note that suffixes do not have meanings of their own; instead they determine the grammatical function of words (eg, think of *big–bigg**est***).
- Support students to learn **a word's associations and grammatical functions**. The best way of learning these is through immersion in and practice with using rich language. However, for English language learners, it can also be helpful to memorise "sample sentences" (Nation 2019).

The following are some general ways to strengthen learning, along with ideas for ways to apply them to your teaching:

- Evidently, the goal of all vocabulary teaching is for students to be able to use new vocabulary fluently and purposefully in speaking, reading and writing. Teachers can best achieve this goal through a combination of explicit instruction and opportunities for meaningful practice (Nation 2019). Have students engage with interesting and authentic texts that include the target words. Occasionally set timed practice activities – such as a 'beat the clock' true or false quiz about target word meanings – to build fluency with word knowledge (Beck et al 2013).
- Be clear and explicit when discussing word meanings. Although dictionary definitions help proficient readers, they can be problematic for beginners: they can be too precise or too vague; include too many pieces of information; or fail to provide for different interpretations of a word. Instead of relying on dictionary definitions, develop your own 'student-friendly' ones. These definitions should capture the essence of the word as it is most commonly used and should be stated in everyday language (Beck et al 2013).
- Repetition is helpful. Encountering the same words across a range of contexts strengthens learning (Nation 2019). Keep a list of words you have taught and find ways to revisit them throughout the year. Consider creating a 'word wall' that the students can refer back to. Make the words moveable (with Velcro dots) so that students can take them to their tables to support their spelling during writing.
- Using visual representations of the words may support students' memory of their meanings. You could use the 'three-dimensional word strategy', in which students define the word, draw a picture of the concept, use the word in context and then find an object to represent it (Wilfong 2021). Another idea is to use online tools such as Google Slides or the Padlet online bulletin board **www.padlet.com**. With these, students can display words with links to images or further information (Nation 2019).
- Plan activities that require deeper processing, helping to make learning 'stick'. Nation describes four different levels of processing that range from shallow to deep: noticing, retrieval, production and elaboration. Certain activities encourage deeper processing. For example, recalling a word's definition requires deeper processing than reading one, and producing one's own definition is deeper still (Nation 2019). You could present a variety of definitions of a word to your students and then challenge them to come up with their own using just three to five words. Alternatively use a 'carousel walk' of words (or

3. TRANSLATION

pictures relating to the words): display the words around your classroom and have groups rotate around the classroom, discussing the meanings of the different words (Wilfong 2021). And of course, use writing to strengthen vocabulary knowledge.

- Help students to make connections between words, creating synapses from already known words to new ones. You could select three words and have students state what is the same about them, what is different and what is a way to remember the individual word meanings. They could complete this in writing, using a graphic organiser. Teaching roots and associated word families is another great way to establish connections (Wilfong 2021).

You can also make use of read-aloud texts to teach vocabulary explicitly. Exhibit 3 sets out one possible routine you could follow.

Exhibit 3: A routine for explicit teaching of vocabulary using read-aloud books

> For this routine, choose books that contain more advanced vocabulary than your students will be reading themselves. Then choose your target words using one of the methods described in the *Selecting words for teaching* section on page 41.
>
> Read the text several times. The first time, read it through with minimal interruptions. Over following readings, stop to provide student-friendly explanations of the target words. You could interrupt a whole text about 8–10 times, or once every 75–100 running words.
>
> When you introduce the target words, first ask students to pronounce the words themselves. Over later readings, facilitate activities to encourage deeper processing. For example, you could get students to:
>
> - provide their own examples of situations or sentences that use each word; for example, for the word *cautiously*, ask, "What other activities might you do cautiously?"
> - act out the word
> - identify examples and non-examples of the word's meaning; for example, for *extraordinary*, ask, "Which of these events could be described as extraordinary …?"
> - finish a sentence that uses the word; for example, for *jealous*, ask them to finish, "I was jealous of my cousin when …"
> - identify sentences containing the word that do, or do not, make sense
> - identify true or false statements that use the word.
>
> Towards the end of the week, when you have worked through all of the target words a number of times, you could review them together with activities such as:
>
> - choosing between the words to match a scenario
> - asking students, "What is the word that means …?"
> - finding things that are the same about the words
> - composing a sentence that uses all the words together.

Source: Adapted from Beck et al (2013) and Biemiller (2012)

3. TRANSLATION

Developing vocabulary by integrating other curriculum areas with writing

We have many opportunities to develop vocabulary knowledge when teaching science or history topics. As you teach knowledge in these other curriculum areas, have students write on the same topics during their writing lessons. Writing, as a productive process, is the ideal way to reinforce new vocabulary (Nation 2019).

The key here is planning. Spend some time thinking about interesting topics for study (and let's be truly child-centred here – perhaps dinosaurs, the solar system, apex predators, the sinking of the *Titanic* or the first Moon landing). Once you have chosen a topic, consider the vocabulary students will encounter and use the three-tier system from Beck and colleagues (2013) to select words (see the *Selecting words for teaching* section on page 41). Then prepare your 'student-friendly' definitions to share.

As you work with new words and phrases, record these for a topic wall – perhaps on moveable cards that students can take to their own desks. Refer to these as you model writing. Also invite your students to refer to them and to use them to support spelling during their own writing practice.

Teaching sentence structure

Having confidence with structuring sentences is key to writing success. Sentences are "the building blocks of all writing" (Hochman and Wexler 2017, p 330) – each one is a contained unit of meaning and sense.

Sentence-writing interventions have demonstrated positive effects on student achievement (Graham and Perin 2007; Saddler and Graham 2005). Learning to re-read and check at the sentence level supports self-regulation – a cornerstone of writing development, according to the Simple View of Writing (Berninger et al 2002). The goal to 'write in perfect sentences', underpinned by the criterion, 'think of an idea, write it down, read it and check it straight away', was shown to be a particularly useful and effective goal in the Fast Feedback intervention study (Walls and Johnston 2021).

We can teach sentence composition informally, by modelling thinking of the sentence, saying it, writing it and re-reading to check. Then we must support our students to also plan, say and (if they are ready) write, read and check (more about this in Chapter 4). At more advanced levels, sentence-combining is the only evidence-based approach to teaching grammar (Saddler 2005).

Teaching sentence structure to very young students

We like to teach five-year-olds about what a sentence is, and to hear the rhythm and phrasing of a sentence, at the end of our daily phonemic awareness lesson (described in Chapter 2).

This is the routine:

- Use toys to teach phonemic awareness and sentence structure. Select three toys to put in a special bag: two have the same sound (your focus for that day) and one does not. For example, on a day when /d/ is the focus, you could include a duck, dog and hammer.
- With the students, segment the words into phonemes, listening for the /d/. Then clap the 'beats' (or syllables) in the words.
- Model thinking of a sentence about one of the toys. For example, say, "I want to think of a sentence about the duck. A sentence is an idea. My sentence is: *The duck can swim*."
- The students repeat this sentence twice, first while clapping the syllables and second by dancing to them.
- The students may share their own sentences about the toys. The class can repeat these sentences while clapping and dancing too.

- If a student has trouble saying a sentence – for example, they just name the subject, "dog" – you could say, "Tell me a whole idea about the dog. What does the dog do (*or* What is the dog like)?"

Note: Thanks to Barbara Brann for the basis of this approach to teaching sentence structure.

Teaching sentence structures using sentence-combining

It is also useful to teach sentence structure more explicitly. Teaching students to label parts of speech, however, is ineffective in improving grammar and can reduce motivation to learn (Saddler and Graham 2005). Instead, use sentence-combining – the only evidence-based approach for teaching grammar (Saddler 2005).

Sentence-combining involves directly teaching about and practising with creating more sophisticated structures by joining two or more simple sentences. You may prompt (or cue) extra words. For example:

You give students two simple 'kernel' sentences (along with the cued words in brackets):

1. *We were swimming.*
2. *A shark came into the bay.* (*and/while*)

Students could form either the compound sentence:

We were swimming and a shark came into the bay.

or the complex sentence:

While we were swimming, a shark came into the bay (Figure 6).

You then ask them to evaluate the different sentence structures.

Figure 6: Sentence-combining to form a complex sentence

You can take sentences from class reading materials or the students' own written work. They could come from new learning in other curriculum areas (eg, science), which has the added benefit of reinforcing new knowledge across the curriculum.

Have students work with a partner to facilitate discussion. The lessons could be entirely discussion-based (ie, students do not necessarily have to write anything down).

Provide opportunities for sentence-combining about twice a week and keep the lessons 'short and sweet' (10 to 15 minutes per lesson is enough).

3. TRANSLATION

Teaching punctuation use

Teach students punctuation use in the context of sentence-combining.

Model correct use during writing time and discuss it.

Teach students to hear the places where they need punctuation by:
- reading to students every day
- re-reading your modelled writing
- using dictation to provide opportunities for practising correct spelling and punctuation use.

Sentence structure and punctuation: knowledge for teachers

To use sentence-combining with our students, we must be confident in our own knowledge of sentence structures and punctuation use. For this reason, here the focus is on teacher content knowledge. But if you already feel confident in this area, skip to page 50 to read more about how you can use our innovative sentence-combining method with students from their first months at school.

Table 3 outlines terms for parts of speech that we use in this section.

Table 3: Parts of speech

Term	Definition	Example
Subject	The doer	*The cat* slept.
Verb	The action	The mouse *ran*.
Object	That which receives the action	Huge waves crashed on *the rocks*.
Noun	The word for a person, place or object	My *brother* was angry.
Pronoun	A word taking the place of a noun	*He* hit *me*.
Adjective	A word to describe the noun	We jumped into the *deep* pool.
Adverb	A word to describe the verb	The monster ate *noisily*.
Coordinating conjunction	A word to join two clauses together	We jumped into the pool *and* I swam to the bottom.
Subordinating conjunction	A word that introduces the non-essential clause in a complex sentence	*While* I was visiting my grandmother, I made a new friend.
Relative pronoun	A word that joins two clauses and acts as the subject or object in the non-essential clause	I made a new friend *who* would change my life forever.

Note: Many words can function as two or more parts of speech, changing their role depending on context. For example, in "The sky is blue", *blue* is an adjective, whereas in "Blue is my favourite colour", it is a noun.

Sentence types and how to write them

In this section we explain the main types of sentences – simple, compound and complex sentences – as well as the descriptive phrases known as appositives. We also set out the main reasons for using each one.

3. TRANSLATION

Simple sentences

A simple sentence contains a subject (a 'who' or doer) and a verb (what they do, the action). It sometimes has an object (that which receives the action). For example:

    We were swimming.   (subject, verb)

    The dog chased the cat.   (subject, verb, object)

The following are some reasons for using simple sentences.

Reason	Example
To state an idea clearly	The kiwi is nocturnal.
To add a sense of urgency or immediacy	Tiredness overtook me. I could not go on.

Compound sentences

To make a compound sentence you join two simple sentences together using a conjunction (*and, or, nor, for, yet, but, so*). The simple sentences become two clauses in one compound sentence. For example:

    We were swimming and a shark came into the bay.

    The dog chased the cat but she was too fast for him.

The following are some reasons for using compound sentences.

Reason	Example
To join two ideas that are related	Night was falling so I quickly built a shelter.
To vary the rhythm of a text	Tiredness overtook me. I could not go on. My mind screamed but my body felt lifeless.

Complex sentences

A complex sentence contains at least two clauses, one of which is essential to the sense of the sentence and the other is less important. You can create a complex sentence in a number of ways. Here we look at three common approaches.

1. Use a subordinate conjunction at the beginning of the sentence.

   > **Subordinate conjunctions** are words that introduce the non-essential clause. They include *after, although, as, because, before, even if, even though, if, in order that, once, provided that, rather than, since, so that, though, unless, until, when, whenever, wherever, whether, while, why*.

   Placing a subordinate conjunction at the beginning of the sentence will make the first clause a subordinate clause (which means it no longer makes sense on its own). For this type of complex sentence, you need to add a comma after the first clause.

   This example uses the subordinate conjunction *while*:

       While we were swimming, a shark came into the bay.

2. Use a subordinate conjunction in between the two clauses. This makes the first clause essential and the second clause non-essential. You don't use a comma between the clauses in this type of complex sentence.

   This example uses the subordinate conjunction *before*:

       We swam to the shore before the shark could come close to us.

3. TRANSLATION

3. Use a relative pronoun in between the two clauses.

> A **relative pronoun** is a word that introduces a second clause and acts as the subject or object in this clause as well. Relative pronouns include: *that, which, whichever, who, whoever, whom, whose, whomever*.

When the relative pronoun introduces a non-essential clause, you use a comma between the clauses. For example:

> The dog chased my grey cat, which had been sleeping in the sun. (relative pronoun = *which*)

When the relative pronoun introduces a clause that is essential to the meaning of the main clause, you don't use a comma. For example:

> You look like the cat that licked the cream. (relative pronoun = *that*)

The following are some reasons for using complex sentences.

Reason	Example
To introduce a sense of mystery or anticipation into a story	Although the house had been empty for some time, we often noticed lights in the attic window at night.
To describe the timing of events	My life changed completely after I moved to the new school.
To compare and contrast	Rather than battle with my sister, I would stay in my bedroom and lose myself in a good book.
To describe cause and effect	Because of underground geothermal activity, parts of the lake are warm.

Appositives

An appositive is a noun or noun phrase that gives further information about a noun or pronoun (the 'who' that is the subject of the sentence). The appositive usually comes just after the noun or pronoun in the sentence, and before the verb. For example:

> The snake, a patient killer, lay in wait for its prey.
>
> Former prime minister John Jelly will be speaking to the school.

In the first example, you need to add a comma on each side of the appositive (*a patient killer*) because it is non-essential to the meaning of the sentence. In the second example, the appositive (*John Jelly*) is essential so you don't need to include commas around it.

The following is the main reason for using appositives.

Reason	Example
To add interesting information about someone or something	The beach, a dark and windswept landscape, made an excellent place for winter adventures.

Tricky punctuation

Some types of punctuation can be confusing or have nuanced rules. Here we focus on speech marks, commas, semicolons and apostrophes.

3. TRANSLATION

Speech marks

You use speech marks around quotations but the tricky part is working out if and how to use other punctuation. This depends on whether the quote is a full sentence and where it comes in the wider text sentence.

Where the **text sentence begins by introducing a quotation**, use a comma or colon. For example:

> The president proclaimed: "It's all lies."
>
> I heard my sister shout, "Where are you?"

As the above examples also show, you use a capital letter at the beginning of a quote that is a complete sentence. You also put the full stop, question mark or exclamation mark at the end, inside the speech marks when it belongs to the quoted material. No other punctuation is needed at the end of the text sentence.

Where the **text sentence continues after the quotation**, add a comma at the end of a quotation. For example:

> "That was a crazy storm last night," said Dad.

When **punctuation belongs to the wider text sentence**, not the quotation, put the punctuation outside of the speech marks. For example:

> He described the city as "horrible".

When **splitting up a quote**, use a comma inside the first closing speech marks. For example:

> "I know you're wrong," she said, "because you never check your facts properly."

Commas

Use a comma after a subordinate clause when it starts a complex sentence. For example:

> After the river went down, we knew we could cross it safely.

Use two commas to separate a non-essential appositive from the surrounding text. For example:

> Ben, an excellent football player, was hoping to play for his national team one day.

Use commas in a list of three or more items in a sentence. For example:

> I like apples, strawberries, pears and bananas.

Use a comma after a transition word at the beginning of a sentence. For example:

> Suddenly, the ground started to shake.

Commas may also be helpful at other times to make the writing clearer.

Semicolons

You can use a semicolon to join two independent clauses (creating a compound sentence) without using a conjunction such as *and*. For example:

> I always eat vegetarian food; animal rights are important to me.

A semicolon can also be useful for listing complex items, where commas could be confusing. For example:

> To write well, students must understand the conventions of genre; the conventions of spelling and punctuation; and the processes of planning, re-reading and revising.

3. TRANSLATION

Apostrophes

Use an apostrophe in a **contraction** to show where the missing letter or letters would go if the words were written in full. For example:

you're, I'm, that's, don't, can't

Use an apostrophe to show **possession**:

- Use *'s* after a singular noun to show that a person or thing owns something. For example:

    That is Emma's pencil.   The school's gala day was a great success.

- Use *s'* at the end of a plural noun to show that people or things own something. For example:

    The teachers' meeting room is here.   The trees' lives depend on us.

- If a plural noun doesn't end in *s*, add *'s* to create the possessive form. For example:

    The women's shoes are on sale.   She was the people's princess.

The apostrophe and *it*: Do not use a possessive apostrophe after *it*. Only use the apostrophe with *it* for the contraction *it's*. For example:

The cat slept on its blanket.   It's a very rainy day.

Sentence-combining for beginners

Dr Christine Braid has developed a system for teaching sentence-combining to beginners. This uses simplified terminology, hand actions and colour coding.

The terminology

Tell students a sentence has a **who** (subject phrase) and a **do** (verb phrase), or else it has a **who** and a **what like**. For example:

The dog (**who**) chases the cat (**do**).

The dog (**who**) is fast (**what like**).

The 'who' may refer to a group or an inanimate object. It may be described using a pronoun (eg, *he, she, it, they*). For example:

Everyone (**who**) is working hard today (**do**).

The computer (**who**) is broken (**what like**). It (**who**) will not start (**do**).

The hand actions

The hand actions are a simple way to represent the sentence parts visually.

Use your right-hand palm up for the **who**, and your left-hand palm up for the **do**.

Students will mirror these actions, so for them, the left palm faces up first and then the right palm follows. In this way, they will be practising left to right directionality for reading and writing.

For a **phrase**, pull your fingers together and move your hand in a horizontal line from left to right.

Signal a **full stop** by making a point in the air with your left index finger.

3. TRANSLATION

The colour coding system

Use coloured cards to represent the parts of the sentence. You can move them during sentence-combining practice to show students different sentence structures. The colour codes are as follows.

The who	The do	The phrase
Coordinating conjunctions (eg, *and, but, so*)		**Subordinating conjunctions** (eg, *while, after, whenever*)

You will also need some cards showing full stops.

Inspiration

You can develop sentence-combining activities out of any experience that interests the students. Toys and picture books are particularly effective.

Using toys

For young students, toys can create a hook into the lesson. For example, you could display a set of undersea creatures or a set of toy vehicles as inspiration for sentence-combining activities.

Using picture books

Choose a high-quality picture book from the list in Chapter 5. Read it and talk about it. Take sentences from the story or construct your own simple sentences about the book.

In some of the examples below, we have taken inspiration from *Clive Eats Alligators* by Alison Lester. The story uses simple sentences throughout but the illustrations add detail and interest that you can make use of during sentence-combining activities.

Management

Keep lessons short. Five minutes may be enough for our youngest students. Use oral practice and then record some of the sentences on the board if you wish.

Work with manageable chunks of knowledge. Perhaps stay with one sentence structure for a few sessions before moving to the next.

Model each new structure as you first introduce it and then have students suggest their own ways of combining or adding to sentences.

The process

The process consists of six stages of increasing complexity. As noted, spend time as needed on each stage for students to build their knowledge before moving on to the next stage.

Stage 1: Introduce the simple sentence and create simple sentences

Start with your inspiration (toys or a book). Tell the students, "We are going to build some sentences about this."

Explain that sentences need a 'who' (subject) and a 'do' (verb). Use the hand signals to show the who, do and full stop.

3. TRANSLATION

Then share sentence examples, inspired by the story.

For example, you might say, "Frank (right palm up) eats muesli (left palm up)" and then make a full stop in the air.

The students repeat the sentence and mirror the actions.

Explain the meaning of the coloured cards: the pink represents the 'who' and the green represents the 'do'.

Represent the sentence using the coloured cards. Put a full stop card at the end (Figure 7). Point to the cards as you say the sentence again.

Repeat this process for other simple sentences.

Stage 1 sentence examples

Inspiration	Who	Do
Sea animal toy miniatures	The shark	swims.
	The sting ray	glides.
Clive Eats Alligators by Alison Lester	Frank	eats muesli.
	Nicki	has a banana.
Stormy weather	The wind	blew.
	The sun	shone.

Figure 7: Simple sentences created using the colour-coding system

Stage 2: Expand simple sentences by adding a phrase

Tell the students, "We are learning to add detail to our sentences."

Lay out the coloured cards and remind them of one of the sentences from Stage 1. Point to the cards as you say the sentence again.

Explain, "We can use a **phrase** to add extra detail to the sentence. This may be a word or a group of words. We can use the phrase to say when, where or how."

Show the yellow cards and explain that these will be for the phrases.

Explain, "The 'who' and 'do' must always stay in our sentence. We can add parts on, but we cannot take away the 'who' or 'do'. The 'who' and 'do' together are called a **clause**."

3. TRANSLATION

Think aloud about the detail you might add to the simple sentence you have chosen. For example, using the pictures from *Clive Eats Alligators*, you might say, "Let's say where Frank eats muesli. Look at the picture. He is at the kitchen table. We can add that information to our 'who' and 'do' sentence (or clause)."

Say a sentence about Frank, using the hand actions for the 'who', 'do' and phrase: right palm up, left palm up, fingers pulling together and moving in a horizontal line to the left. Then show the index finger full stop.

Build the sentence using coloured cards (Figure 8). Point to the cards as you say the sentence again.

Later in the lesson, you can show the students that we can add more than one phrase (for recording, note that these phrases are separated by commas). The table includes some examples of these.

Stage 2 sentence examples

Inspiration	Who	Do	Phrase(s)
Sea animal miniatures	The shark	swims	in the deep ocean.
	The stingray	glides	silently and peacefully, through the sparkling water.
Clive Eats Alligators by Alison Lester	Nicky	has a banana	in tiny bites.
	Frank	eats muesli	before school, at the table, with his dog by his side.
Stormy weather	The wind	blew	all night long, outside my window, like a monster.
	The sun	shone	like a diamond.

Figure 8: Beginning to expand simple sentences

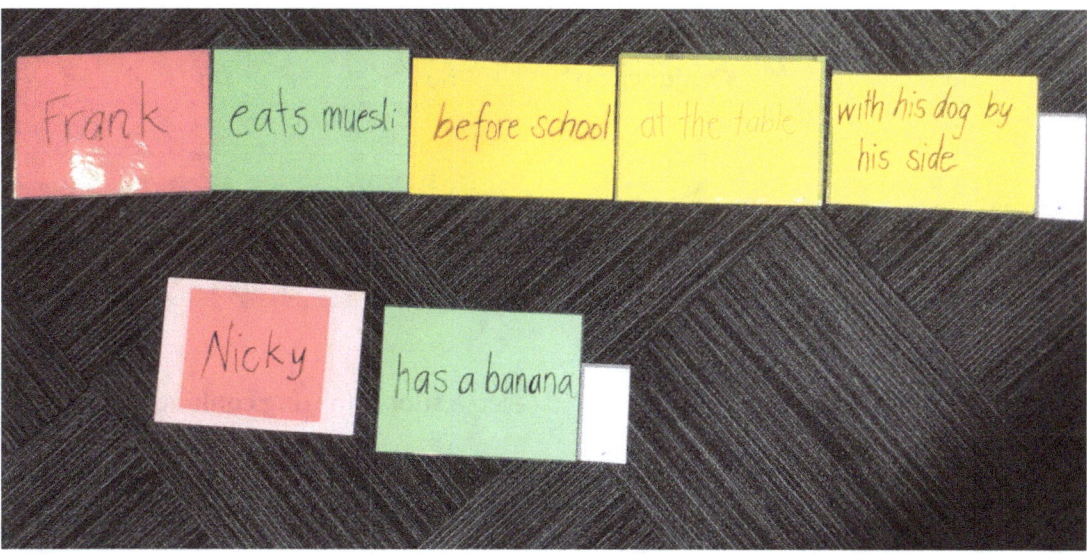

Stage 3: Move the phrases around

Now show the students that phrases can come before the clause too.

Move the coloured cards to visually represent the new structure. Point to the cards as you say the sentences (note that a comma is needed after the phrase when it comes before the clause).

© Essential Resources Educational Publishers Ltd

3. TRANSLATION

Even though some of the examples below feel like sophisticated structures, they are still simple sentences because they consist of just one clause (containing one 'who' and one 'do').

Stage 3 sentence examples

Inspiration	Phrase	Who	Do	Phrase
Sea animal toy miniatures	Sleek and dark,	The shark	swims	in the deep ocean.
	Through the sparkling water,	The sting ray	glides	silently and peacefully.
Clive Eats Alligators	Every morning,	Frank	eats muesli	at the kitchen table, with his dog by his side.
	Under her favourite tree,	Nicky	has a banana	in tiny bites.
Stormy weather	Like a monster,	the wind	blew	all night long, outside my window.
	In the morning,	the sun	shone	like a diamond.

Stage 4: Create compound sentences

Explain to the students, "We can join two simple sentences together using special words called conjunctions. The simple sentences will now become two clauses in one compound sentence."

Show the dark-blue card and explain that it represents these joining words – the conjunctions.

Lay out two simple sentences in cards, with full stops at the end of each. Say the sentences and point to the cards. Then take away the full stop at the end of the first sentence, replace it with a conjunction card and discuss the change. Say the new compound sentence, pointing to the cards.

Stage 4 sentence examples

Who	Do	Conjunction	Who	Do
The shark	swims.		The stingray	glides.
The shark	swims	and	the stingray	glides.
Frank	eats muesli.		Nicky	has a banana.
Frank	eats muesli	but	Nicky	has a banana.

Stage 5: Create complex sentences

Explain, "We can join the clauses using a special joining word called a **subordinating conjunction**. This word will make one of the clauses feel unfinished."

Show the light-blue card and explain that it represents this special joining word – the subordinating conjunction.

Say a sentence and lay it out in colours (Figure 9).

3. TRANSLATION

Stage 5 sentence examples – subordinating conjunction in between

Who	Do	Subordinating conjunction	Who	Do
The stingray	hides	when	the shark	comes near.
Frank	eats muesli	while	Nicky	has a banana.

Stage 5 sentence examples – subordinating conjunction at start

Subordinating conjunction	Who	Do	Who	Do
Whenever	the shark	comes into the lagoon,	the stingray	hides.
Although	Frank	eats muesli,	Nicky	has a banana.

Figure 9: Using a subordinating conjunction to combine sentences

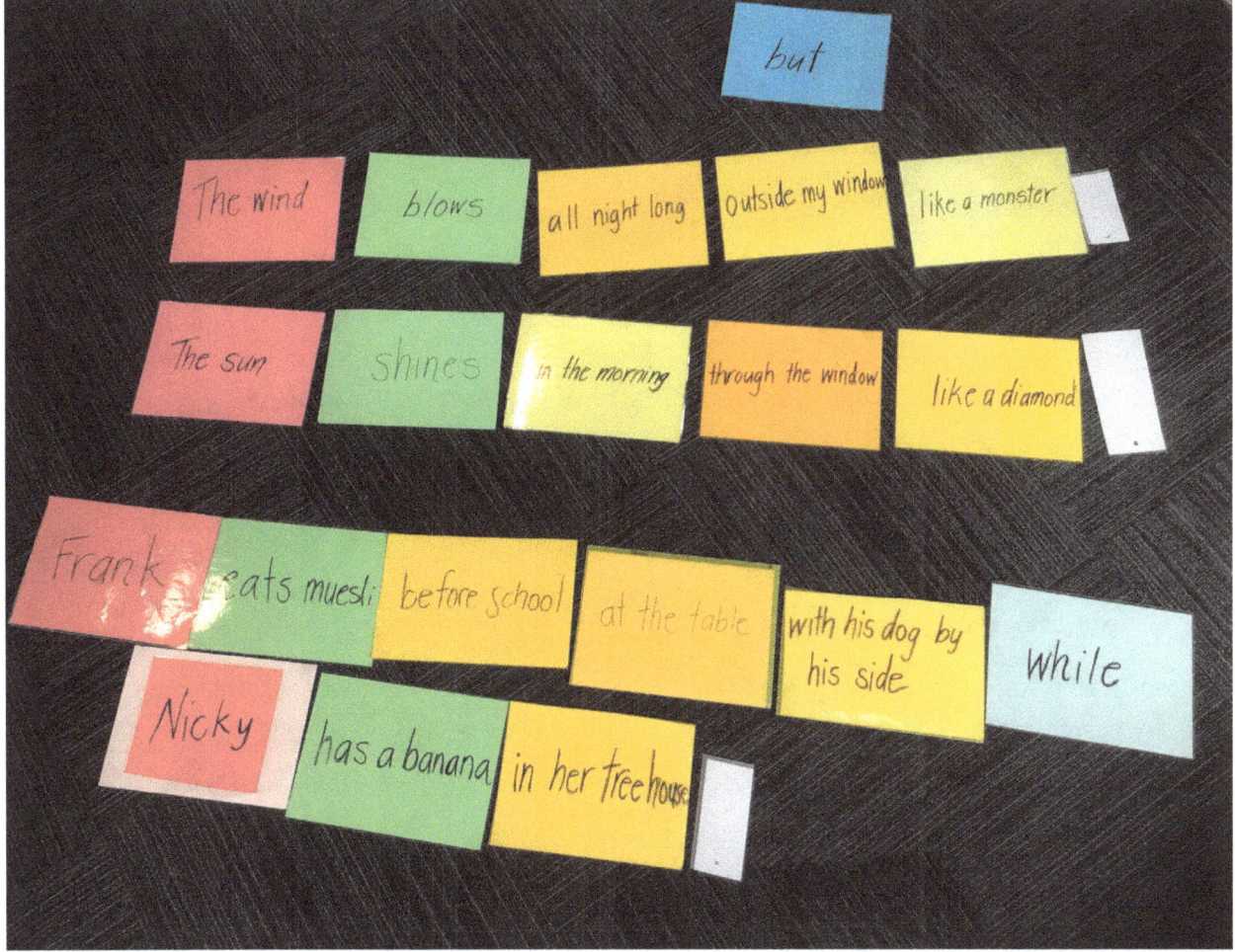

Stage 6: Continue to explore possibilities

Continuing to work with sentences like this, you could end up working with some sophisticated structures.

For example, you might produce compound sentences with many phrases (clauses are in italics):

Every morning, *Frank eats muesli* at the kitchen table, with his dog by his side but *Nicky has a banana* in tiny bites under her favourite tree.

The wind blew all night long and *it destroyed the garden shed*.

3. TRANSLATION

You might also come up with complex sentences that have many phrases (clauses are in italics):

While *Frank eats muesli* at the kitchen table, with his dog by his side, *Nicky eats a banana* in tiny bites under the trees.

Even though *the wind blew* like a monster, all night long, in the morning *the sun shone* like a diamond.

You could show students how to insert a phrase between the 'who' and the 'do' (but don't jump into this too early as it could be confusing for some).

Stage 6 sentence examples

Who	Phrase	Do	Phrase
The shark,	sleek and dark,	swam	silently into the lagoon.
The sun,	like a diamond,	shone	through my bedroom window.

You could also deconstruct compound or complex sentences, finding the clauses and turning them back into simple sentences. For example:

The wind blew. It blew all night long. It blew outside my window. It blew like a monster.

Build reflection into your sentence-combining lessons

Reflection may improve the quality of students' revisions.

Ask students to reflect on the impact of the new sentences and choose the sentence they like best.

Tell students, "You are the author and you have the choice."

Helping students to apply their knowledge during writing lessons

Teach students to use different sentence structures intentionally, and not just to please the teacher or marker. Refer to Stage 4 of our scope and sequence, which will encourage an intentional approach. For example, you could select the goal, "To use a complex sentence to introduce a sense of mystery into my story", and then provide examples such as:

Whenever I walked past the old house, a shiver went down my spine.

You can use the 'who, do' terminology to prompt correct or interesting sentences during student planning time. For example, "Can you add a phrase to tell me more about that?"

You can feed back to students using this terminology too.

Dealing with common errors with sentence structure

The following are some common errors students make in writing sentences, as well as suggestions for responding to them.

1. The student does not use a full stop at the end of a sentence.

Example: The dog was lost in the forest he was looking for his family.

Say, "The dog was lost. This has a 'who' and a 'do'. It is a sentence so you can put a full stop at the end. He was looking for his family. This has a 'who' (he) and a 'do', so it is another complete sentence."

2. The student uses a comma at the end of a sentence.

Example: I didn't come to school yesterday, I was sick.

Say, "Here are two complete, simple sentences. They both have a 'who' and a 'do'. You need to put a full stop at the end of the first sentence. Another way you can do it is to join the two together with a conjunction. Then they will become clauses in one compound sentence."

3. The student is reluctant to put a full stop after a short sentence.

Example: The man ran he was racing to get to the bus.

Say, "'The man ran' is a complete sentence. It has a 'who' and a 'do'. You can put a full stop after *ran*."

4. The student puts a full stop at the end of a clause in a complex sentence.

Example: The children ran away from the monster. Who was chasing them.

Say, "*Who* is a joining word. Just put one full stop at the very end of the two connected ideas."

Example: When we got to the beach. The sun was shining.

Say, "*When* is a joining word – even though it comes at the beginning of the first clause. The word *when* is joining your first idea to your next idea so just put a full stop at the end of the two ideas."

5. The student puts a full stop at the end of a clause and then adds a phrase.

Example: The children collected wood. On a sunny day.

Point to the phrase and say, 'This part is not a complete sentence because it has no 'who' (subject) or 'do' (verb). That means it needs to be connected to the sentence before it. You can rub out the full stop and write *on* with a lower case *o*."

Students can write compound and complex sentences from the first year at school

Do not constrain the writing of younger students by requiring them to always write in simple sentences. Notice how these younger students often speak in complex sentences – for example, "When my dog went missing, I cried."

So if younger students want to write a complex sentence, support them to do it. We want students to know that writing is about expressing their original, interesting and amazing ideas.

What to do about commas

Because using commas is complex, it can be sensible to hold off on explicit instruction around this – until you see that students are using capital letters and full stops correctly (and consistently).

A solution: Until students are ready, you could co-construct comma use with them. For example, if the student writes a complex sentence that requires a comma, add the comma yourself and say, "This is an amazing sentence structure. It needs a comma. I'll show you how to use these yourself very soon."

4. The writing lesson

Two essential components of the writing (composition) lesson are formative assessment and feedback. Formative assessment is essential for targeted teaching. Feedback is powerful for all learning but may be especially important for writing as it enhances students' self-awareness, which is integral to self-regulation. In a meta-analysis of feedback interventions for writing, Graham and colleagues (2015) calculated that the effect size was 0.87 for adult feedback, 0.62 for self feedback and 0.58 for feedback from peers, while the effect was less substantial (0.38) for feedback from computers. Feedback information is made even more powerful when combined with a visual display of progress (Fuchs and Fuchs 1986).

In this chapter, we look at how you can make Fast Feedback an effective part of your writing lesson (Figure 10). This set of methods for formative assessment, teaching and feedback has been demonstrated to have positive effects on achievement and motivation, and can be used by busy teachers to accommodate a range of learning needs (Walls and Johnston 2021).[2]

Figure 10: Two samples from a Year 4 boy on the Fast Feedback trial

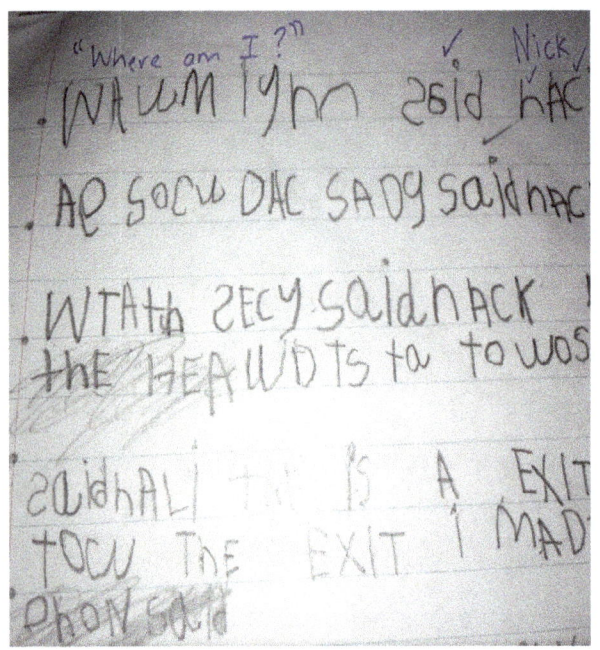
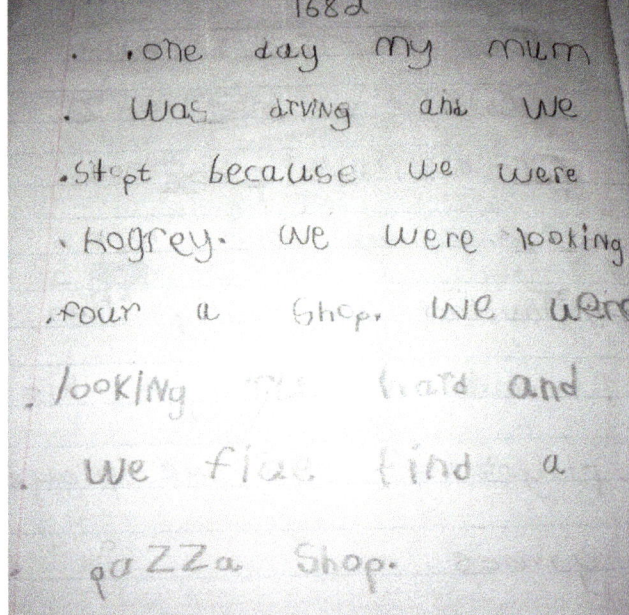

These samples were written just 10 weeks apart.

How to use Fast Feedback

1. Select a goal for each student

Assess each student's writing to select one specific learning goal (you can use our scope and sequence to help with this – see the final section of this chapter). Ask yourself, "What is the next small step that will make the writing more readable, or the writing process more manageable, for this student?"

This goal will become the primary focus for the student until they have mastered it. Record it in the back of the student's book. Use the wording: "(Student's name) is learning to …"

---

[2] I am immensely grateful to the teacher who is the original creator of Fast Feedback. I first saw her model the method in 2003, while watching a Harry Hood video, *The Management of an Independent Writing Programme*, which I had borrowed from my school. Unfortunately, I have been unable to acquire a copy of the video in recent years. When I asked Harry, he could not recall her name but believes she must have been teaching at Abbotsford School in Dunedin, New Zealand in the early 1990s. If this teacher or anyone who recognises her from this description would like to contact the publisher, please do so and future editions will provide due acknowledgement.

4. THE WRITING LESSON

While you will select goals based on individual student needs, groups of students in your class will usually have similar needs and will therefore have the same goals. Generally, around three goals will be operating in a class at any one time.

2. Teach to the goals

Discuss and model the goals every day. Prompt and praise for these skills during supported writing (see the *Key components of a writing lesson* on page 60 for a more in-depth description of these lesson structures).

3. Provide targeted feedback, using the Fast Feedback conference

The Fast Feedback conference takes 30 seconds per student and has three parts:

(a) Praise the ideas expressed in the writing. For example, "You wrote about the shark's sharp teeth. How exciting!"

(b) Acknowledge any step of progress towards the goal. For example, "You are learning to leave spaces between words and you did this (some of the time/with help/all of the time) today. Great work."

(c) Turn to the back of the student's book and record either: the date and a tick for partial achievement, or achievement with support; or the date and a sticker for consistent and independent achievement. Figure 11 illustrates this approach over a number of days.

When a student has achieved at least five stickers in a row, it may be time to select a new goal. Say, "You have been learning (to leave spaces between words) and you are doing it every day. Fantastic work. I think it's time to choose a new goal." Then, with the student sitting beside you, turn to the next page at the back of the student's book and record the new goal.

Figure 11: Visual tracking system

The back page of a student's writing book, showing the visual tracking system for the goal, "To leave spaces between words."

4. THE WRITING LESSON

Why Fast Feedback works
We recommend Fast Feedback for many reasons:

- Selecting one priority goal for each student gives you a strong sense of purpose during writing lessons. You know what to model, what to prompt for during the student's practice time and (of course) what to feed back on.
- Having one priority goal gives the students a sense of security too. They know from the start of the lesson what you will be checking on and they know that they will receive some positive feedback for the effort they make (we celebrate ticks, as well as stickers).
- Students can focus on the feedback when you present it succinctly, supported by the visual display.
- The display of ticks and stickers is a way of proving to students that they can learn. We hope to activate a 'positive feedback loop'. That is, the students see their ticks turn into stickers and they begin to believe in themselves. They become more motivated and make greater effort. This leads to faster progress and yet more positive feedback.
- The visual display encourages teacher reflection too. If you see ticks for too many days in a row or inconsistency with stickers being followed by ticks, ask what more you can do to support the student to achieve. Perhaps you need to reconsider the goal, sharpen your modelling or provide closer support to the student during their writing practice time.

Key components of a writing lesson
The four essential parts of a writing lesson are:

1. modelling for 5–10 minutes
2. student planning for 5–10 minutes
3. supported writing for 25–45 minutes
4. feedback for 10–20 minutes.

How long you spend on each part of the lesson will vary depending on the age and stage of your class.

Teach writing every day to support all students to be successful.

Modelling
Your model needs to be as succinct and clear as possible. A model of one or two sentences is long enough for students in Year 1. Never write more than about six sentences, even for senior students (model just one paragraph of a longer text).

Use a dark pen and large, clear script, visible to all students.

1. Introduce the purpose and express enthusiasm.
   Say, for example, "We are writing stories. Our stories need to be fun for ourselves and for our readers. I thought today we could write stories with an interesting and mysterious setting – under the sea, in the deepest part of the ocean."

2. Remind students of their learning goals.
   Say, for example, "While we are writing, we are practising our learning goals. Some people are learning to write real words. Some people are learning to leave spaces between words."

3. Begin to write, thinking aloud to plan each sentence.
   Say, for example, "I want to write a story about a shark. My first sentence is: 'The shark has sharp teeth.'"
   Explicitly model each relevant goal, at least once during the session.
   Explicitly model spelling strategies, at least once during the session. For this, invite the students to help you to segment the words into sounds and then ask them to tell you which letters to write. Encourage a choral response – with all the students' voices together – to support maximum engagement and to maintain pace.
   Remember to re-read and check each sentence as you go.
   Invite your students to read with you. Say, "My sentence sounds the way I want it to sound. It has a capital letter at the beginning and a full stop at the end."

4. Re-read and check the whole text at the end of writing.
   Make a positive evaluative statement. Say, for example, "I am proud of my writing. It is exciting. I wrote real words and I left spaces between my words."

Student planning strategies

Across all levels, use think–pair–share:

1. At the end of the modelling session, say, "I have had my turn to write. Now it's your turn. Close your eyes and think of an idea. When I say 'Go', turn to the person next to you and practise saying your first sentence to them. Then listen so that they can practise saying their sentence to you too."
2. Give students one minute to think. Then say, "So, I want to hear good talking now ... Go."

For young students, and students who struggle, get them to practise saying their sentence to you too. After telling a friend their sentence, these writers should come to you and say it again. In response, say something encouraging about their idea, remind them of their learning goal and give them their book and a pencil.

To manage this routine in a junior class (where lots of students will need close support), you may wish to set up some play-based fine-motor activities for half the class, while the others talk and write, and then swap the groups over. Independent activities could include drawing, cutting, pasting, chalkboard writing, writing on whiteboards, playing with pegs, threading and using play-dough.

For more advanced students, written planning is useful. Use one of the planning templates at the end of this chapter. You may need to model the use of these at the beginning of any new unit. Send students to their tables to complete the plan and move among them to support their planning and to keep them on track. Consider setting a time limit for this initial planning phase (5–10 minutes).

Supported writing (student practice time)

Learning to write is like learning to ride a bike – we learn by doing it. So having daily student practice time is important. Move quickly among your students to give everyone the support they need. Focus on the Fast Feedback goals and support spelling too.

The following are some ways you can support students to progress towards their goal:

- Remind them of their goal if they have forgotten or praise them when you see them practising the skill.
- Use an eraser to help them to make tidy corrections (eg, if they have forgotten to leave a space or to use a capital letter at the beginning of a sentence).
- Praise them for re-reading and checking whenever you see them doing so.

- Praise them when they are motivated to make appropriate corrections or revisions and ask for the eraser.
- Praise focus and quiet writing.

To support students' spelling, you must first **know your spellers**. The following strategies are also useful:

- When a student is unsure of a word, prompt them to segment it into sounds and to think of letters for the spelling patterns you have already taught them.
- For patterns they do not yet know, just show them the pattern (or the whole word). Write it at the top of their page or on a Post-it for them to copy.
- Following this routine, scribe as the student tells you which letters to write. In this way, you can get the word down quickly, before moving to the next student who needs help.
- For more advanced writers, encourage them to use a dictionary for a few words each day. Online dictionaries work well.
- Create a class chart of topic-specific vocabulary that students can refer to during a writing unit.

Feedback

Remember that the lesson always ends with feedback, using the Fast Feedback structure.

Frequently asked questions

Should I have writing groups?

Ability-based writing groups are not necessary because writing is an independent process. However, splitting your class into two groups can allow you to give close support to a smaller number of students.

How often should I conference with students?

The Fast Feedback conference is the fulcrum on which you can strengthen all teaching and learning, and it should inform your planning for the following day. Aim to use it at least twice each week, with every student in your class.

How do I get through all the students in my class?

While Fast Feedback conferences occur as the final structure in a writing lesson, you may be able to spread these out over a longer period. You may find that relatively early on in the lesson, some students have written enough to demonstrate progress towards or consistent achievement with their Fast Feedback goal so you could conference with them at that stage.

Also keep the conferences short at 30 seconds per student. This allows for regular conferencing, but also keeps your message succinct.

Should students use erasers?

Use erasers in your modelling and teach your students to use them. For beginning writers (and writers who have not used erasers before), you can hold the eraser. As students begin to write with some confidence and fluency, they may be ready to have their own eraser.

Erasers help students to make tidy corrections and to keep their writing readable. This is important for developing habits of re-reading, checking, and correcting or improving work. Most students want to present work that looks tidy. As an eraser allows them to do this, it can add to their motivation to write.

Finally, according to empirical models of the writing process, we do not simply draft, and then check and revise. Instead, we write and revise continually and recursively, in what Flower and Hayes (1981) have described as a "juggling act". Erasers support this process, as they allow students to make changes 'on the go'.

Should I encourage invented spelling?

The benefit of invented spelling is that it requires students to analyse sounds in words. However, what if students cannot do this well? Or what if they do not yet have the knowledge of spelling patterns to be able to record the sounds correctly?

If these issues are not addressed early on, some students will practise incorrect spellings for too long. If this becomes a habit, it can be difficult to break.

Another problem is that some students are reluctant to invent spellings – they don't want to guess and make a mistake.

Instead of invented spelling, use co-constructed spelling. This means you will encourage students to apply the knowledge they do have and show them the rest of the words they ask for help with.

What if a student wants to write about a different topic, or write in a different genre from the one I have modelled?

Let them – some of the time. Writing can be a wonderful way for students to experience autonomy and to practise self-expression. However, they also need opportunities to extend their knowledge of text types and vocabulary. For this reason, writing on the same free-choice topic every day is not optimal for writing development.

Should I correct and mark my students' writing?

Do not make corrections in pen beside a student's own work or cross out anything in their book. Instead, if you would like something to be corrected, support students to do this themselves.

A teacher's penned corrections on student work can make the page harder to read. Students are not likely to learn from such corrections. In a worst-case scenario, all they communicate to a student is that something was wrong.

You could, however, use ticks as a form of positive feedback (eg, to highlight the correct spelling of a difficult word or correct use of sentence punctuation).

You may wish to highlight something special, such as effective use of metaphorical language.

Scope and sequence

The following is a scope and sequence for writing goals for primary (elementary) students, aligned with approximate spelling stages and suggested year levels. These are intended to be taught and practised with close support from the teacher, and in the context of meaningful writing tasks. The goals reflect current research in writing development (see Graham et al 2012) and have been trialled in the New Zealand context (Walls and Johnston 2021).

The sequence of goals has been divided into four stages. The first two stages focus on technical fundamentals, and the third and fourth stages focus on writing for a purpose.

4. THE WRITING LESSON

At Stage 1, students learn to say a sentence before writing, write 'real' letters and words, and leave spaces between words. When practising these goals, students write just one sentence each day.

Stage 2A is for students to develop their concept of a sentence and practise a process of writing and checking as they go. Students write two or three sentences each day.

At the end of Stage 2A, you must check that students are developing the basic skills, without confusion. For students who are demonstrating difficulty, Stage 2B may be useful. These goals address common confusions that should be remedied as early as possible.

The broad aim of Stage 3 is to give students interesting and meaningful purposes within which to practise the basic skills they have just mastered. It contains two simple sets of goals for narrative and expository text. Once students are demonstrating some fluency with writing at least a few sentences every day, they are ready for Stage 4.

Stage 4 includes many goals, targeting three skill sets:

1. organisation and paragraphs
2. sentence structures and punctuation
3. language and style.

Goals at this stage are grouped according to three purposes: narrative, expository and persuasive. Stage 4 will equip students with a range of writing strategies, which they will use with purpose and self-awareness, in the context of meaningful writing tasks. While the goals in Stages 1–3 are numbered and should be taught and practised in sequence, Stage 4 goals do not need to be taught in any particular sequence. You should select from them according to the specific needs of the students in your class and the contexts for writing you wish to cover in any given term.

You can use the assessment checkpoints at the end of each set. The guide ends with a list of possible contexts.

Overview of this scope and sequence

Stage	Focus	Page
1	Beginning to compose and transcribe	65
2A	Writing in sentences, re-reading and checking	66
2B	Addressing difficulties and confusions	67
3	First steps into genre	68
4	The writer's toolbelt	70
1–4	Suggested contexts for writing at all four stages	74

4. THE WRITING LESSON

Stage 1: Beginning to compose and transcribe

Goals	Expectations	Spelling	Timeframes
1. To say a sentence before writing	Teacher will support students to plan (by saying a sentence) and to write one sentence each day.	For code knowledge, see Unit 1 of the *Spelling made simple* programme (Chapter 2).	New Entrant/Year 1
2. To write some real letters and words	Students will put a full stop at the end.	Students will begin to apply this knowledge.	Begin this stage about three months after school entry, when students have sound-letter knowledge and letter formation skills for all short vowel and single consonant sounds.
3. To leave spaces between words	Teacher will support students to read the sentence, pointing to each word. Teacher may scribe the entire sentence for those students working on goal 1, and most of the sentence for students working on goal 2.	They will begin to spell some irregular high-frequency words: *I, the, is, my*.	Work on this stage for three to six months, or until all three goals are achieved consistently and independently.

Stage 1: Assessment checkpoint

At the end of Stage 1 ...	Examples of progress over Stage 1
• Can the student write a single simple sentence that is readable? • Are they recording all the sounds in single-syllable words, with no sounds missing or added? • Can they write some longer words, with support? • Are they forming letters correctly? • Are they leaving spaces between words?	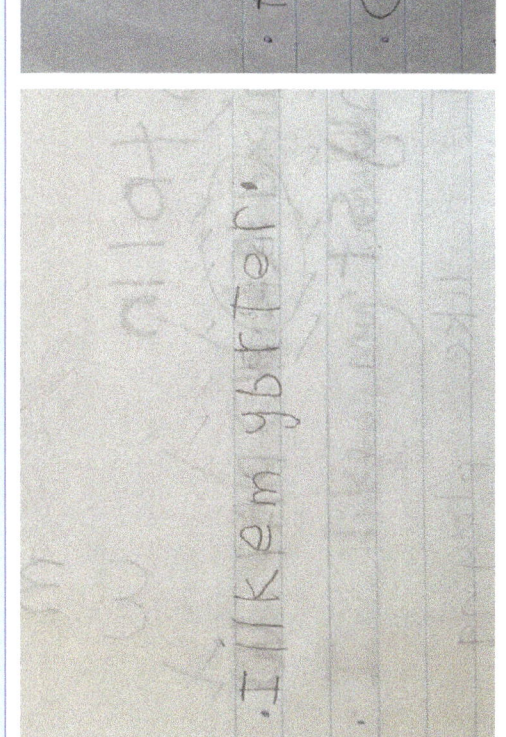

4. THE WRITING LESSON

Stage 2A: Writing in sentences, re-reading and checking

Goals	Expectations	Spelling	Timeframes
1. To write two sentences each day 2. To re-read and check every sentence • Think of an idea. • Write it. • Read it and check it straight away. • Check that it sounds the way I want it to sound. Check that it has a capital letter at the beginning and a full stop at the end.	Students will be supported to plan and write two or more sentences each day. Students will plan by saying each sentence to a teacher or buddy, or quietly to themselves. When beginning goal set 2, students will use full stops at the end of every sentence. At the end of goal set 2, students will use a capital letter at the beginning of every sentence and a full stop at the end. Teacher will support students to read and check every sentence as they write; and will support them to re-read and check the whole text at the end of writing.	For code knowledge, see Units 2 and 3 of the *Spelling made simple* programme (Chapter 2). Students will continue to require close support with spelling. Remind them to apply the knowledge they have. Show them the spellings of more advanced words and word parts. Students will spell an increasing number of irregular high-frequency words: *we, to, going, was, they*.	Years 1 and 2 Work on this set for three to six months. Consolidate all the Stage 1 and 2 skills before moving on to Stage 3.

Stage 2A: Assessment checkpoint

At the end of Stage 2A …	Examples of progress over Stage 2A
Can the student write two or more simple sentences about a topic? Is the student using correct sentence punctuation? Is the student re-reading and checking every sentence as they write? Is the student able to spell single-syllable words? Are they able to record most sounds in multisyllabic words? Is their letter formation correct and fluent? Note: If you notice any difficulties with layout, letter formation or spelling, do not continue to Stage 3. Address difficulties and confusions as early as possible, using Stage 2B's goals 3, 4 and/or 5.	hollow tongue The halwha his a hollo tongue. The tonyiw is big. Note: The sample on the right is the work of an older student who needs practice with the goal "to re-read and check every sentence". This can be a useful goal for older students who make errors with sentence structure and punctuation. I am having trouble with maths and I would like some help and some help with reading writing

4. THE WRITING LESSON

Stage 2B: Addressing difficulties and confusions

Goals	Why?	Other actions	Expectations, spelling and timeframes
1. To leave **big** spaces between words	This goal is for students whose spacing is inconsistent, leading to problems with readability.		Continue with the expectations for Stages 1 and 2A. Continue to work on these goals until the difficulties have been resolved. Use plenty of specific and positive feedback. Acknowledge any steps in progress towards the goal. Use varied and meaningful writing tasks and respond positively to the student's ideas, as well as their persistence with the technical aspects of writing. *Examples of progress over Stage 2B*
2. To check the formation of the letter(s) _____	This goal is for students who are not yet secure with forming particular letters. You could use it to target forming a single letter (eg, *d*) or a group of letters with the same formation pattern (eg, letters with sticks first, then tunnels – *h, n, m*).	Handwriting instruction is essential for all junior students. This goal is a sign that you should strengthen your handwriting teaching for the student.	
3. To spell thoughtfully • Slow down. • Copy common words from a word checking card (see template 4.1, page 75). • Listen to the sounds in other words. • Then check with a teacher.	This goal is for students whose spelling attempts demonstrate a lack of knowledge of sound–letter correspondences (they cannot apply knowledge from Stages 1 and 2A). It is also for students who demonstrate difficulty with hearing sounds and syllables.	Spelling instruction is essential for all students. This goal is a sign that you should strengthen your spelling instruction for the student. Word cards are not necessary for all students. They may be useful for students who repeatedly spell common words incorrectly. If you use them, have cards for irregular high-frequency words, with a limited number of target words. The layout must be clear and uncluttered.	

Stage 2B: Assessment checkpoint

After working on Stage 2B, return to Stage 2A: Assessment checkpoint to re-evaluate the student's readiness for Stage 3.

© Essential Resources Educational Publishers Ltd

4. THE WRITING LESSON

Stage 3: First steps into genre

3A Narratives: Our writing needs to be fun and interesting, for ourselves and for our readers.
3B Reports: When writing scientific reports, or when recounting a special event, our writing needs to be true, clear and interesting.

3A Goals	3B Goals	Expectations	Spelling	Timeframes
1. To include a story-problem	1. To include only factual or true information	Students will write several sentences each day, creating a coherent piece of writing, one or two pages in length. They will plan by talking to a teacher or buddy, or by using a simple written template. They will write in sentences, with correct punctuation, reading and checking as they go.	For code knowledge, see Units 3 and 4 of the *Spelling made simple* programme (Chapter 2). Students will continue to need close support with spelling. Remind them to apply the knowledge they have. Show them the spellings of more advanced words and word parts. They will spell an increasing number of irregular high-frequency words.	Years 2 and 3 Work on Stage 3 goals for about six months. Work on each genre for at least four weeks at a time. Alternate genres so that you cover each one twice a term. Consider using the final week of each term for something different: poetry or letter-writing.
2. To describe the setting (what it looks, sounds and feels like) so that your reader gets a picture in their mind	2. To use the first sentence to introduce the topic and then add other sentences with more detailed information	Students at this stage will continue to need teacher support. Prompt them to practise the specific goal they are working on; and remind them to read, check and correct. As students begin to write more, it is important that they are able to make tidy corrections and keep their writing readable. You could carry an eraser to help students with any corrections. When students demonstrate that they know what to attend to in revision, you could give them their own erasers. If you are not using erasers, show students how to make tidy corrections. Use one line for deletions. Keep markings to a minimum and keep the page 'clean'.		
3. To describe a main character (the way they look and behave) so my reader can imagine them	3. To use precise or scientific words when they are needed to make the meaning clear			

68 © Essential Resources Educational Publishers Ltd

4. THE WRITING LESSON

Stage 3: Assessment checkpoint

At the end of Stage 3, check …	Examples of progress over Stage 3
• Can the student write several sentences fluently? • Can they write in perfect sentences, reading and checking as they go? • Are they noticing errors and are they motivated to make tidy corrections? • Can they write for different purposes, including stories, recounts and reports? • Are they beginning to use a range of techniques to meet the purpose of the writing?	Elephants Elephants are not New Zealand animals. They are not native to New Zealand. Elephants are mammals They are native to a different country on earth. looking ed factory • I was in the abandonedfactory. I was looking at a toy machine. It was making a doll. It looked like me.

© Essential Resources Educational Publishers Ltd

4. THE WRITING LESSON

Stage 4: The writer's toolbelt

Genre and purpose	4A Narrative text Our writing needs to be fun and interesting, for ourselves and for our readers.	4B Reports and explanations (See template 4.2, page 76.) When writing scientific reports or recounting a special event, our writing needs to be true, clear and interesting.	4C Persuasive writing/expressing an opinion (See template 4.3, page 76.) We are writing to express our opinion on a topic and to explain our reasons why.
Skill areas	Goals	Goals	Goals
Planning, organisation, paragraphs	Use a story-web (template 4.4, page 77) to plan. Include a setting, characters, problem, action and ending. Introduce the setting and characters in the first paragraph, and then introduce the story-problem. *Then try:* Hook the reader into the story by introducing the problem or action in the first paragraph.	Use a tactile planning template (template 4.5, page 75) or a graphic organiser to plan the whole text and then each paragraph before writing. Organise my writing into paragraphs. Present information in a logical order. Use the introduction to tell the reader what they will be learning about and to convince them it is worth reading about. Use the paragraphs after the introduction for further information and details. Include a topic sentence at the beginning of each paragraph to introduce the main idea of the paragraph. Use the conclusion to summarise the main ideas. *Then try:* Use the conclusion to suggest a question for future research and leave the reader feeling inspired to learn more.	Express an opinion orally while participating in a small-group or whole-class discussion. Use graphic organisers to plan the whole text and each paragraph before writing. Use the introduction to present your argument and get the reader interested in the topic. Use the paragraphs after the introduction to provide evidence for your argument. Include a paragraph that presents other arguments and the evidence for them. Include a conclusion that inspires the reader to think and learn more.

continued ...

4. THE WRITING LESSON

Genre and purpose	4A Narrative text	4B Reports and explanations	4C Persuasive writing/expressing an opinion
Skill areas	**Goals**	**Goals**	**Goals**
Sentence structures	Use some simple sentences to create a sense of urgency and drama: "I felt sand under my feet. I would not drown. I was alive." Use a complex sentence to describe the timing of events: "While we were swimming, a shark came into the bay." Use a complex sentence to add a sense of mystery: "Whenever I passed the old house, a shiver went down my spine." Use an appositive to describe a character, or something in the setting: "The steep cliffs, survivors of weathering by storm and sea, looked far too treacherous to climb." Include a range of simple, compound and complex sentences to add interest and vary the rhythm of my language.	Use some simple sentences to express ideas clearly: "Water is a liquid." Use some compound sentences to join related ideas: "Ice is a solid and water vapour is a gas." Use some complex sentences to describe cause-and-effect relationships: "Because tōtara wood is very hard, these trees were often used to build waka." Or: "Our school field floods whenever there is heavy rain." Use an appositive to add information about the subject of a sentence: "Kiribati, an island nation in the Central Pacific, is extremely vulnerable to sea-level rise."	Use a statement to express your opinion clearly and simply: "Swimming is an important life skill." Include a rhetorical question (a question with an obvious answer) to make a point: "Just 35% of New Zealand's rivers are clean enough to swim in. Are we really 'clean and green'?" Use some simple sentences for clarity. Use some compound sentences to join related ideas. Use some complex sentences to compare and contrast ideas, to explain cause-and-effect relationships or to describe the timing of events.

continued ...

4. THE WRITING LESSON

Genre and purpose	4A Narrative text	4B Reports and explanations	4C Persuasive writing/expressing an opinion
Skill areas	Goals	Goals	Goals
Language and style	Choose to write in either the first person (*I*) or the third person (*he, she, they*). Be consistent throughout the story. Write in the past tense throughout the story. Use transition words and phrases to sequence and connect main events: *It all started when; The first sign of trouble was; After some time; First; Next; Then; Later that day.* Use vivid nouns and verbs, ones that are memorable, unusual or specific: *pōhutukawa* instead of *tree; raced* instead of *ran*. Describe the setting, using the five senses: sight, sound, smell, taste and touch. Describe the characters: their looks, behaviours and the way they feel inside. Use a simile to add interest to my description of the setting or a character: "The mountain appeared before us, as fearsome and still as a sleeping giant." Use alliteration to describe how the setting sounds: "The wind whispered in the grasses." Use onomatopoeia to describe the sounds of the setting: *Thump!* Use direct speech to add excitement to the story: *"Help!"*. Use direct speech to show how characters are feeling: *"Don't leave me here!"*	Include a useful title. Include only factual information. Use precise language to express ideas clearly. This may be scientific, technical or topic-specific language. Use the third person for scientific or historical reports. Use the first person when recounting a personal experience. Use transition words to connect ideas: *First; In addition; In particular; In conclusion.* Use transition words to sequence and connect events: *First; Next; Then; Later on; Finally.* When listing related items, use a comma to separate each item.	Use the first person. Use inclusive language (*we, our*) to get my reader 'on side'. Use a personal story or some emotive language to engage your reader. Provide facts and evidence for my argument. I can introduce these facts with transition words: *For example; To illustrate; For instance; The evidence is clear.* Support my argument with a quote from an expert. Use quotation marks correctly. Explain why the quote is relevant. Use transition words to connect ideas: *First; In addition; Finally; In conclusion.* Use transition words and phrases to signal I am moving to a new or different argument: *However; On the other hand; Even though; But.* When listing related items, use a comma to separate each item.

4. THE WRITING LESSON

Stage 4: Expectations, spelling, timeframes and assessment

Expectations	Spelling	Timeframes
Students will plan and write at least one paragraph each day.	For code knowledge, see Units 4–8 of the *Spelling made simple* programme (Chapter 2) or the scope and sequence of your chosen spelling programme (eg, the knowledge items listed in Liz Kane's *The Code* for Years 4–6).	Years 4–6
They may spend two to three days completing a text.		This stage contains over 50 goals. Students should practise each one for at least a week at a time and re-visit it in a number of different contexts.
They will plan using think-pair-share and in writing form, using graphic organisers.	Students will need support to apply this knowledge to their writing.	**Examples of progress over Stage 4**
Students will read and check every sentence as they write, making tidy corrections as they go.	Show them the spellings of words they do not yet have the knowledge to spell correctly.	
At the end of writing, students will read the whole text and check on their progress towards the selected goal.	When writing on a topic over several days, create a class chart of topic-specific words that students can see from their tables and refer to during writing time.	
Students will evaluate the overall impact of their writing, and how well they have achieved their purpose for writing. They will do this individually or with a buddy, and could use a graphic organiser for self or peer assessment (see templates 4.6–4.8, page 78).	Students could begin to use online and hard-copy dictionaries. To use these successfully, they will need to be able to hear and record just the first few sounds in a given word.	

Assessment
Throughout Stage 4, check:

- Can the student use a specific writing strategy independently?
- Can they use it with awareness? For example, when learning to include a complex sentence to describe a cause-and-effect relationship, can they show you this sentence in the text they have written and explain its purpose?
- Are they using this strategy effectively? Does it add impact to their writing? If not, why not?
- Are they overusing a particular strategy?
- Once students are applying a given strategy consistently and independently, they can begin to work on a new learning goal.
- If students are struggling with a particular strategy, strengthen your teaching and give them more support during practice time. Or 'slice back' to work on a simpler strategy.

© Essential Resources Educational Publishers Ltd

4. THE WRITING LESSON

Suggested contexts for writing at all four stages

Stages 1 and 2

Animal stories, eg, *The dog can run.*

(Cute) spooky stories, eg, *The ghost is in the house.*

Animals of the sea, eg, *The shark is big.*

Weather reports, eg, *The sun is hot.*

Problems with pets, eg, *I lost my dog. I looked for him at the park.*

Stage 3A: Narratives

Stories with real-life story problems. Model text: *Maisie, Charlie and the Wobbly Tooth* (Lucy Cousins).

Stories set under the sea. Model text: *Te Manu the Tekoteko* (Ron Bacon).

Stories with (not-so-scary) monsters or witches. Model texts: *The Witch in the Cherry Tree* (Margaret Mahy); *The Gruffalo* (Julia Donaldson).

Stage 3B: Reports

Base writing around your current class topic such as: The water cycle; The solar system; Native trees, birds or insects; Cultural celebrations; Jobs people do; Local roadworks that students can visit and talk about.

Stage 4A: Narratives

Retelling traditional stories, myths and legends.

Writing animal stories for younger students to teach them about the animal in the context of a story that is fun to read. Model texts: *The Very Hungry Caterpillar* (Eric Carle); *The Cay* (Theodore Taylor); *Hatchet* (Gary Paulsen).

Writing stories with animals that can speak. Model texts: *The Kuia and the Spider* (Patricia Grace); *Charlotte's Web* (EB White).

Writing survival stories. Model texts: *The Cay* (Theodore Taylor); *Hatchet* (Gary Paulsen).

Writing a made-up diary of a quirky character. Model text: *The Diary of a Wimpy Kid* series (Jeff Kinney).

Stage 4B: Reports and explanations

Writing to explain aspects of the context for a class novel. Historical novels work well. For example, when reading *An Elephant in the Garden* (Michael Morpurgo), students could write about the bombing of Dresden in 1945.

Writing biographies of local adults with an interesting story to tell. Students could interview their subjects first.

Writing useful information for school visitors and displaying it in the school office. For example, students could create pamphlets to tell visitors about the native trees and plants on the school grounds.

Writing to share learning for any current class inquiry.

Recounting an interesting event at school.

Recounting a time when the student felt particularly sad, excited, angry or afraid. They could practise some narrative writing techniques to add interest.

Stage 4C: Persuasive writing

Warm up with less serious topics: Cats make better pets than dogs; Learning to swim is more important than learning to read; Students should be allowed phones at school.

Then select a topic of deeper relevance to the students, such as an in-school issue (eg, changing a system or rule, or allocating funds for a new resource); or a local community issue (eg, water quality at a local beach or river and ways to improve it).

Use your current class inquiry as a context for this kind of writing and research the topic thoroughly before asking students to express an opinion on it.

4. THE WRITING LESSON

Graphic organisers

Template 4.1: Word checking card

a	b	c	d	e
after again are away	beautiful because by	can't come coming	day do down	every everyone

f	g	h	i	j
first for from	go goes going	have here how	(ant)	(jam)

k	l	m	n	o
(kite)	like look looking	made more my	now	of one other out our

p	q	r	s	t
people	(queen)	(rabbit)	said saw she some	the there their they

u	v	w	x	y	z
(umbrella)	(violin)	want was were when	(x-ray)	you your	(zebra)

© Essential Resources Educational Publishers Ltd

4. THE WRITING LESSON

Template 4.2: Report writing plan

Topic: _____ Title: _____

Introduction
Conclusion

Template 4.3: Persuasive writing plan

Topic: _____ Title: _____

Introduce your argument
Provide reasons or evidence
Describe other arguments
Restate your argument – explain why it is superior to other arguments
Conclusion: summarise your argument

4. THE WRITING LESSON

Template 4.4: Story-web

Title: _____

Setting		Characters
	Problem	
	Action	
	Ending	

Note: Thanks to Hilton Ayrey for the basis for this activity.

Template 4.5: Tactile planning

Topic: _____ Title: _____

Cut out the five paragraph outlines. Make notes using key words and phrases. Staple the outlines together as a booklet.

Introduction
-
-
-

Conclusion
-
-
-

Subtopic: _____
-
-
-

Subtopic: _____
-
-
-

Subtopic: _____
-
-
-

Note: Thanks to Barbara Brann for the basis for this activity.

Template 4.6: Narrative writing buddy check

Writer: _____ Reader: _____ Date: _____

Does the writing have characters, a setting and a problem?   ☺ or ☹

Is the story fun and interesting to read?   ☺ or ☹

Positives:

Advice:

Template 4.7: Report writing buddy check

Writer: _____ Reader: _____ Date: _____

Is the writing clear?   ☺ or ☹   Is the writing interesting?   ☺ or ☹

Positives:

Advice:

Template 4.8: Persuasive writing buddy check

Writer: _____ Reader: _____ Date: _____

Does the writing state arguments clearly?   ☺ or ☹

Does it provide reasons or evidence?   ☺ or ☹

Positives:

Advice:

5. Contexts for writing and teaching about genre

In this chapter, we begin with an overview of purposeful writing tasks that apply to teaching any genre, before covering relevant teacher knowledge, including for teaching specific genres – narrative texts, reports and persuasive writing. To close the chapter, we summarise our recommended picture books that will be an asset in your writing programme.

Purposeful writing tasks

Setting writing tasks that are purposeful is essential for every writing genre.

Set writing tasks that are interesting and extending

Writing tasks need to be interesting and extending. Integrate learning from other curriculum areas so that students get to write on topics that take them beyond the limits of their own imagination.

Be truly child-centred in your choices. What topics would excite a primary age student? Our 'go to' science-based topics include dinosaurs, volcanoes, the solar system, apex predators and extreme weather. Or students could write about moments in history – the sinking of the *Titanic* or the first Moon landing. Another idea is to explore the context of a class novel – set in a different time (such as Michael Morpurgo's *An Elephant in the Garden* or Theodore Taylor's *The Cay*). For narrative writing, explore the story setting: write stories set under the sea, in a dark forest, in a future world or in an old, abandoned house.

Show students that we write for a purpose

Students need to know that writing can be used for a variety of purposes, and that we write with this in mind. More authentic tasks will support intentional writing (McCutcheon 1988). For example, the task "Write the biography of a local war veteran, to be published in the school newsletter" may encourage students to consider purpose-related goals such as to write in clear, interesting ways and treat the material respectfully. A task such as "Write about what you did in the holidays" is less likely to inspire such thinking.

Teach knowledge of genre and text structures

We need to explicitly teach knowledge of different genres, including conventions of style and structure. Stay with one type of writing for a few weeks but plan for many different tasks to keep the learning interesting. Support students to plan for these different text types and, later, to evaluate their work. Other activities may also be useful, such as having students analyse model examples, or rewrite texts using a different structure from the original (Reynolds and Perin 2009).

Teacher knowledge for teaching genre

Here we look briefly at the different conventions and structures of three genres. We also cover how you can support students to develop their skills with paragraph writing and planning their writing.

Narrative text

Conventions of style. Stories usually include a setting, characters and a problem. They can be imaginary or based on a real-life experience. They need to engage the reader.

5. CONTEXTS FOR WRITING AND TEACHING ABOUT GENRE

Stories can be written in the first person (*I*) or the third person (*he, she, they*). They are usually written in the past tense. The writer must be consistent throughout.

The writer describes the setting and characters to help their readers imagine them. Useful descriptive techniques for this purpose include metaphorical language, specific nouns (eg, *the old oak* instead of *tree*), and – in conveying sounds – alliteration and onomatopoeia.

Transition words and phrases help to sequence the story:

> Examples
> *It all started when … The first sign of trouble was … After some time … Later that day … Meanwhile …*

Using direct speech helps bring the story to life.

Structure. Approaches to structuring narrative stories include:

- introducing the setting and characters first, then introducing the problem, before moving on to describe the action and finally the ending
- introducing the problem or action in the very first paragraph to 'hook the reader in'.

Reports

Conventions of style. Scientific or historical reports use third person. When recounting a personal experience, the writer may use first person.

Many reports use precise language. For example, a report about the water cycle may include words such as *water vapour* and *precipitation*.

Report writers find transition words and phrases useful to connect ideas.

> Examples
> *First … In addition … In particular … In sum … To conclude …*

Structure. A report starts with an introduction. This tells the reader what they will be learning about and engages them with the topic. The following paragraphs provide further information and details.

The report should end with a conclusion. Here, the writer may summarise the main ideas covered and/or present a question for future research.

Persuasive writing

Conventions of style. A piece of persuasive writing may be written in the first person.

The writer often uses inclusive language to get the reader 'on side'.

> Examples
> *We must … For the sake our future …*

The writer may use a personal anecdote or emotive language to engage the reader.

They include evidence – facts and data – to support the argument. Some introductory phrases help to flag such evidence.

> Examples
> *For example … To illustrate … For instance … The evidence is clear: …*

The writer may quote from an expert.

Transition words can either:
- connect ideas: *First; In addition; Demonstrably; Clearly; Significantly, Evidently*
- signal a new or different argument: *However; On the other hand; Although*.

Structure. Persuasive texts begin with an introduction that presents the argument and engages the reader. The following paragraphs provide evidence supporting the writer's argument.

One paragraph should present arguments different from the point of view the writer is arguing for, and the evidence for them.

The text should finish with a conclusion that inspires the reader to think and learn more. This may highlight an interesting point already made or present a question for future research.

Paragraphs

A paragraph should be at least three sentences long for beginning writers. It could begin with a topic sentence, introducing the main idea of the paragraph. The following sentences add more detailed information about that topic.

In some well-written paragraphs, a topic sentence may not be entirely obvious. In these cases, the sentences work together to convey meaning and the main idea is implied.

From a teaching perspective, it may be counterproductive to get too fussy over the paragraph structure. Think about the writer's purpose and evaluate the strength of the paragraph in relation to this. If the student is writing a report, for example, ask yourself: is the information presented in a clear, coherent and logical way?

Student planning for different text structures

1. Use graphic organisers for planning and for peer evaluation:
   - Model their use.
   - Support students as they create their own plans.
   - If planning is challenging, choose a planning goal from the Fast Feedback scope and sequence (see Chapter 4).

2. Teach tactile planning as a flexible strategy that will work for any genre:[3]
   - Give students five small pieces of paper (or Post-it notes) to plan a five-paragraph report, story or opinion piece.
   - Students record subtopics at the top of each piece of paper.
   - They add key words and phrases, for detail, below each subtopic heading.
   - They order the pieces of paper into a booklet, from the piece on paragraph one at the top of the pile and so on through to the piece on paragraph five at the bottom. They staple the papers together and refer to the booklet as they write. For some students, tearing off each page as they finish a paragraph reinforces a sense of self-efficacy and motivation (Brann 2001).

---

3 Thanks to Barbara Brann for this technique.

5. CONTEXTS FOR WRITING AND TEACHING ABOUT GENRE

3. Use a human continuum to generate ideas for persuasive writing topics:[4]
   - Write a statement on the class whiteboard – for example, "Learning to swim is more important than learning to read".
   - Display four opinion cards – *Strongly agree, Agree, Disagree, Strongly disagree* – at different points across a classroom wall in this order so that the strong opinions are at opposite ends of the wall.
   - Tell students to think about their level of agreement with the statement and their reasons for this response. Then ask them to move to stand by the card that indicates their level of agreement. Ask them to move without talking.
   - When students have found their places on the continuum, invite them to share their reasons for agreeing or disagreeing with the statement. After hearing from a few students, give everyone an opportunity to change where they are standing.

Using picture books for writing

In a writing programme, picture books are incredibly useful for teaching text structure, sentence structures, and conceptual and vocabulary knowledge. They also provide inspiration for the students' own writing.

Here are some titles we recommend, with notes as to how you may use them with your classes.

For juniors

Clive Eats Alligators, Alison Lester. This book follows seven friends through their day. It uses simple sentences that make perfect 'kernel' sentences for sentence-combining activities. The illustrations provide the detail.

The Squiggle, Carole Schaefer. While walking with their class, a student finds a piece of string and uses it to create imaginary creatures. You could use this book to explore vocabulary (*a big scaly dragon*) or the way that alliteration can convey a sense of sound and magic (*slither slish*). Students could create their own string images and write about them.

Maisy, Charlie and the Wobbly Tooth, Lucy Cousins. Charlie the crocodile must go to the dentist. His friends support him and the dentist, Mr Biteright, is kind. This story could provide inspiration for the students' own stories about going to the dentist or their stories with animal characters.

Dogger, Shirley Hughes. Dave's favourite toy is accidentally sold at a school fair but his sister Bella saves the day. The story is engaging, with a clear problem that is resolved through the initiative of children. The illustrations are fascinating in their detail and their expressive qualities. Students could write their own stories about losing something precious.

Harry the Dirty Dog, Gene Zion. Harry runs away from home and plays in the coal. He gets so dirty that he changes from a white dog with black spots to a black dog with white spots, and when he gets home, his family does not recognise him. This story, with a clear problem and (joyful) resolution, is engaging for students and could inspire more stories about dogs. Other ideas you could suggest for dog story problems are: dogs go missing; they get into fights; they get hurt and need to go to the vet; stray dogs need to find a home.

My Many Coloured Days, Dr Seuss. Enjoy classic Seuss verse with richly painted illustrations. Use this book to talk about feelings, and to explore rhyme and figurative language.

---

4 Thanks to the tutors at the New Zealand Graduate School of Education for this technique.

5. CONTEXTS FOR WRITING AND TEACHING ABOUT GENRE

The Very Hungry Caterpillar, Eric Carle. You could use this children's classic as a starting point for learning about the life cycle of a butterfly and about the names of the days of the week. The illustrations and language are beautiful: "In the light of the moon, a little egg lay on a leaf." Students could write their own stories about animals and what they do on each day of the week. They could write simple reports about the life cycle of a butterfly.

For all ages

My Cat Maisie, Pamela Allen. Andrew experiences excitement, hope, disappointment and finally friendship in this story about finding a pet. You could use this for practice with story retelling, for finding the moment where Andrew changes or for exploring how pictures convey meaning. Link it to other pet stories such as Lauren Child's *I Want a Pet* or Gillian Shields' *Dogfish*.

The Hidden Forest, Jeannie Baker. This story has a conservation theme. The illustrations are beautiful and unique, created using collage. Students could explore changes in the main character, Ben. They could examine sentence construction and language use. They could write their own conservation-themed stories and illustrate them using collage too.

Wilfrid Gordon McDonald Partridge, Mem Fox. A young boy asks his elderly friends, "What is a memory?" They provide a range of answers, sometimes with simile (*as precious as gold*). Use this text to explore themes of ageing and friendship, and the concept of memory. Ask students to explain what memory is, using their own words. Ask them to think of their own similes to help explain the meaning of the word.

The Snow Lambs, Debi Gliori. This is a story of friendship between a boy and his dog. Use it for retelling and for exploring key elements of narrative structure, including the problem and resolution. Students could retell or rewrite this story from the point of view of the dog.

The Kuia and the Spider, Patricia Grace. A kuia (old woman) and a spider argue about whose weaving is best and then whose grandchildren are best – seemingly unaware of their exquisite seaside backdrop. This story juxtaposes elements of mystery with the everyday. It could provoke discussion about animals and people, and what animals can do better than us. It could inspire new stories about animals and people living together and talking to each other.

Rose Meets Mr Wintergarten, Bob Graham. This story is a version of Oscar Wilde's *The Selfish Giant*. Mr Wintergarten is feared by the neighbourhood children until Rose forms a connection with him. The cartoon-style illustrations are dynamic and colourful. You could use this text to explore story structure and for story retelling. Students could discuss the characters, their emotions and how they solved the story problem.

Little Mouse's Big Book of Fears, Emily Gravett. Little Mouse tells us about their fears, explaining terms such as *arachnophobia* in a child-friendly way. You could use this story to discuss the students' own fears, or to explore the meanings of these challenging words – all of which contain the Greek root *phobia*.

Te Manu the Tekoteko, Ron Bacon. The people from under the sea take Te Manu down to their house under the waves, but Rua saves him. This traditional Māori story invites us to compare driftwood – shaped by the ocean – to carvings, shaped by human hands. You could use it for story retelling, or to inspire new stories set under the sea.

Owl Moon, Jane Yolen. A child and father go on a night-time adventure to look for owls. Explore Yolen's strategies for describing the story setting. Her structures and language are haunting: "Somewhere behind us, a train whistle blew, long and low, like a sad, sad song."

5. CONTEXTS FOR WRITING AND TEACHING ABOUT GENRE

The Witch in the Cherry Tree, Margaret Mahy. David and his mother are baking cakes when a witch comes down to perch in their cherry tree, "like a wicked black parrot". The witch tries to steal David's cakes, but he outsmarts her. Use this story to talk about what is real and what is imagined, and to explore story structure and the use of figurative language.

For older students

The House that Jack Built, Gavin Bishop. The words of the familiar childhood rhyme have been re-interpreted, with the illustrations conveying new meanings. This book explores themes of colonisation in the New Zealand context. Link it to *The Rabbits* by John Marsden (see below).

Voices in the Park, Anthony Browne. The story of a visit to the park is told from the perspectives of four different characters. The words and pictures interplay to convey meaning. Use this text to explore the personalities, thoughts and emotions of the different characters. Discuss the strategies the author has used to describe them.

Meanwhile, Jules Feiffer. Feiffer plays with conventions of the comic book and, in particular, of the word *meanwhile*, which can be used to instantly transport the reader to different places and events. Students could write to add new *meanwhile* moments to the story. They could write their own stories, using *meanwhile* as a transition word.

The Fisherman and the Theefyspray, Paul Jennings. A fisherman must decide what to do when he catches a rare fish. The language and illustrations are dramatic and engaging. You could use this book as a provocation for persuasive writing: Should the fisherman release the fish or keep it? Why?

The Rabbits, John Marsden. This story explores colonisation in the context of Australia. The text is simple and at times stark, while the pictures are vivid and dramatic. Use this text to explore themes of colonisation and power, or descriptive writing strategies, such as the use of personification and evocative language ("many grandparents ago"). You could used this story alongside *The House that Jack Built* by Gavin Bishop (see above).

Rules of Summer, Shaun Tan. This story has mysterious political undertones. Siblings help each other in a strange and threatening world. Students could explore detail in the illustrations. They could talk about rules, power relationships and loyalty. They could write their own stories, using the same format and starting, "This is what I learnt last summer …".

Luke's Way of Looking, Nadia Wheatley. Luke sees things differently from other people. As he learns to accept himself, others begin to accept him too. You could use the story to prompt discussions around individuality, creativity, artistry and authorship. Students could write their own stories about challenging times with friends. Tell them that they could base these stories on real life or make them up (so that they don't feel too self-conscious in undertaking this task).

First to the Top: Sir Edmund Hillary's Amazing Everest Adventure, David Hill. This tells the story of Sir Edmund Hillary and Tenzing Norgay as they become the first climbers to reach the summit of Mt Everest. Use this book to teach students about that moment in history and then have them write their own reports. You could use the text to extend students' knowledge of certain concepts and vocabulary – such as the dangers of climbing at altitude, and the need for climbers to carry oxygen. It could inspire further study of the Himalayas or the history and culture of Nepal as well.

Weekly plan for spelling

Term: _____ Week: _____

Learning objectives

Sound:

Spelling possibilities:

Pattern or rule for the week:

Day 1: Creating a list

Prepare word lists for the range of spelling possibilities. Highlight the word list for the week.

Day 2: A focus on word meanings

Choose two to three words. Choose one meaning-based activity to work on with your class. (Use the routine plan for guidance.) Prepare an example.

Day 3: Elkonin boxes

Choose two to three words. How many sounds are in each word? Prepare an example in Elkonin boxes.

Day 4: Heart words in Elkonin boxes

Choose a heart word. How many sounds does it have? Record it in Elkonin boxes and highlight the 'heart part'.

Day 5: Dictation

Prepare one or two sentences for a whole-class dictation.

References

Allcock, J. 2008. *Switch on to Spelling*. Porirua: MJA Publishing.

Applebee, A. 1984. Writing and reasoning. *Review of Educational Research* 54(4): 577–596

Arfé, B, Festa, F, Ronconi, L and Spicciarelli, G. 2021. Oral sentence generation training to improve fifth and 10th graders' writing. *Reading and Writing* 34: 1851–83.

Bach, D. 2014. UW prof: Handwriting engages the mind. *UW News*. URL: www.washington.edu/news/blog/uw-prof-handwriting-engages-the-mind/ (accessed 14 February 2023).

Beck, IL, McKeown, MG and Kucan, L. 2013. *Bringing Words to Life: Robust vocabulary instruction*. New York, NY: Guilford Press.

Biemiller, A. 2009. *Words Worth Teaching: Closing the vocabulary gap*. Columbus, OH: SRA/McGraw-Hill.

Biemiller, A. 2012. Teaching vocabulary in the primary grades: vocabulary instruction needed. In J Baumann and E Kame'enui (eds) *Reading Vocabulary: Research to practice*. New York, NY: Guilford Press.

Berninger, V. 1999. Coordinating transcription and text generation in working memory during composing: automatic and constructive processes. *Learning Disability Quarterly* 22(2): 99–112.

Berninger, V, Graham, S, Vaughan, K, Abbott, R, Begay, K, Byrd Coleman, K, Curtin, G and Minch Hawkins, J. 2002. Teaching spelling and composition alone and together: implications for the Simple View of Writing. *Journal of Educational Psychology* 94(2): 291–304.

Brann, B. 2000. *The Magic Caterpillar Story: A handwriting programme to reinforce correct letter formation*. Darling Heights, QLD: Merganza Training and Development.

Brann, B. 2001. *Working with Students with Learning Difficulties*. Darling Heights, QLD: Merganza Training and Development.

Ehri, L. 1989. The development of spelling knowledge and its role in reading acquisition and reading disability. *Journal of Learning Disabilities* 22(6): 356–65.

Flower, L and Hayes, J. 1981. A cognitive process theory of writing. *College Composition and Communication* 32(4): 365–87.

Fuchs, L and Fuchs, D. 1986. Effects of systematic formative evaluation: a meta-analysis. *Exceptional Children* 53(3): 199–208.

Graham, S and Harris, K. 1997. It can be taught, but it does not develop naturally: myths and realities in writing instruction. *School Psychology Review* 26(3): 414–24.

Graham, S and Harris K. 2014. Fostering budding writers. *Observer* 27(7). URL: www.psychologicalscience.org/observer/fostering-budding-writers (accessed 14 February 2023).

Graham, S and Hebert, M. 2010. *Writing to Read*. New York: Carnegie Corporation.

Graham, S and Perin, D. 2007. A meta-analysis of writing instruction for adolescent students. *Journal of Educational Psychology* 99(3): 445–76.

Graham, S, Berninger, V, Abbott, R, Abbott, S and Whitaker, D. 1997. Role of mechanics in composing of elementary students: a new methodological approach. *Journal of Educational Psychology* 89(1): 170–82.

Graham, S, Harris, K and Fink, B. 2002. Contribution of spelling instruction to the spelling, writing, and reading of poor spellers. *Journal of Educational Psychology* 94(4): 669–86.

REFERENCES

Graham, S, Bollinger, A, Olson, C, D'Aoust, C, MacArthur, C, McCutcheon, D and Olinghouse, N. 2012. *Teaching Elementary School Students to Be Effective Writers: A practice guide*. (NCEE 2012-4058.) Washington, DC: National Center for Educational Evaluation and Regional Assistance, Institute for Education Sciences and US Department of Education.

Graham, S, Hebert, M and Harris, K. 2015. Formative assessment and writing: a meta-analysis. *The Elementary School Journal* 115(4), 523–47.

Graves, MF, Brunetti, GJ and Slater, WH. 1982. The reading vocabularies of primary grade children of varying geographic and social backgrounds. In JA Niles and LA Harris (eds), *New Inquiries in Reading Research and Instruction* (pp 99–104). Rochester, NY: National Reading Conference.

Henry, M. 2003. *Unlocking Literacy: Effective decoding and spelling instruction*. Baltimore, MD: Paul Brookes.

Hochman, J and Wexler, N. 2017. One sentence at a time. *American Educator* Summer: 30–43.

Hoover, WA and Gough, PB. 1990. The simple view of reading. *Reading and Writing* 2(2): 127–60.

James, K and Englehardt, L. 2012. The effects of handwriting experience on functional brain development in pre-literate children. *Trends in Neuroscience and Education* 1: 32–42.

Jones, D and Christensen, C. 1999. Relationship between automaticity in handwriting and students' ability to generate written text. *Journal of Educational Psychology* 91(1): 44–9.

Jones, A, Wardlow, L, Pan, S, Zepeda, C, Heyman, G, Dunlosky, J and Rickard, T. 2006. Beyond the rainbow: retrieval practice leads to better spelling than does rainbow writing. *Educational Psychology Review* 28(2): 385–400.

Joshi, M, Treiman, R, Carreker, S and Moats, L. 2008. How words cast their spell. *American Educator* Winter: 6–8, 10–13, 16, 42.

Kent, S, Wanzek, J, Petscher, Y, Al Otaiba, S and Young-Suk, K. 2014. Writing fluency and quality in kindergarten and first grade: the role of attention, reading, transcription, and oral language. *Reading and Writing* 27: 1163–88.

Kilpatrick, D. 2016. *Equipped for Reading Success: A comprehensive, step by step program for developing phoneme awareness and fluent word recognition*. Syracuse, NY: Casey and Kirsch.

Kirschner, P, Sweller, J and Clark, R. 2006. Why minimal guidance does not work: an analysis of the failure of constructivist, discovery, problem-based, experiential, and inquiry-based teaching. *Educational Psychologist* 41(2): 75–86.

Lane, HB and Allen, SA. 2010. The vocabulary-rich classroom: modelling sophisticated word use to promote word consciousness and vocabulary growth. *The Reading Teacher* 63(5): 362–70.

Marulis, LM and Neuman, SB. 2010. The effects of vocabulary intervention on young children's word learning: a meta-analysis. *Review of Educational Research* 80(3): 300–35.

McCutcheon, D. 1988. 'Functional automaticity' in children's writing: a problem of metacognitive control. *Written Communication* 5(3): 306–24.

McCutcheon, D. 1996. A capacity theory of writing: working memory in composition. *Educational Psychology Review* 8(3): 299–325.

McGaw, B, Louden, W and Wyatt-Smith, C. 2020. *NAPLAN Review: Final report*. State of New South Wales (Department of Education), State of Victoria (Department of Education and Training) and Australian Capital Territory.

Ministry of Education. 2021. *How Our Education System Is Performing for Literacy: Progress and achievement of New Zealand learners in English medium settings*. Wellington: Ministry of Education.

Moats, L. 1998. Teaching decoding. *American Educator* Spring/Summer: 1–9.

REFERENCES

Moats, L. 2010. *From Speech to Print: Language essentials for teachers* (2nd edn). Baltimore, MD: Paul Brookes.

Nagy, W, Herman, P and Anderson, R. 1985. Learning words from context. *Reading Research Quarterly* 20(2): 233–53.

Nation, P. 2019. The different aspects of vocabulary knowledge. In S Webb (ed), *The Routledge Handbook of Vocabulary Studies*. London: Routledge.

Pondiscio, R. 2015. *The 57 Most Important Words in Educational Reform* [video]. URL: **www.youtube.com/watch?v=WKSIRXa6OLk** (accessed 18 January 2023).

Pulido, L and Thériault, P. 2022. Manuscript and/or cursive: the contribution of research conducted since 2012 on handwriting instruction. *Journal of Occupational Therapy, Schools, & Early Intervention*. DOI: 10.1080/19411243.2022.2084487 (accessed 7 January 2023).

Ray, A and Graham, S. 2019. Effective practices for teaching students who have difficulty with writing. *Learning Difficulties Australia* 51(1): 13–16.

Reynolds, G and Perin, D. 2009. A comparison of text structure and self-regulated writing strategies for composing from sources by middle school students. *Reading Psychology* 30: 265–300.

Saddler, B. 2005. Sentence-combining, a sentence-level writing intervention. *The Reading Teacher* 58(5): 468–71.

Saddler, B and Graham, S. 2005. The effects of peer assisted sentence-combining instruction on the writing performance of more and less skilled young writers. *Journal of Educational Psychology* 97(1): 43–54.

Stone, L. 2021. *Spelling for Life: Uncovering the simplicity and science of spelling* (2nd edn). New York, NY: Routledge.

Tunmer, WE and Chapman, JW. 2012. The simple view of reading redux: vocabulary knowledge and the independent components hypothesis. *Journal of Learning Disabilities* 45(5): 453–66.

Van Cleave, W. 2019. *Morphology Matters: Building vocabulary through word parts*. URL: **www.wvced.com/wp-content/uploads/2019/04/Morphology-Matters-4-1-19.pdf** (accessed 16 January 2023).

Walls, H and Johnston, M. 2021. The Fast Feedback method: a quasi-experimental study of the use of formative assessment for primary students' writing. *Australian Journal of Learning Difficulties* 26(1): 21–46.

Wilfong, LG. 2021. *Vocabulary Strategies that Work*. New York, NY: Routledge.